LOOSE LIPS SINK SHIPS

LOOSE LIPS SINK SHIPS

Tales From The Waters

FELICIA S HARGROVE

Image of Faith FSH
LLC

Image Of Faith FSH, LLC

CONTENTS

IMAGE OF FAITH, LLC
PO BOX 741927
RIVERDALE, GA 30274
ISBN: 979-8-9860288-0-4 (PAPERBACK)
ISBN: 979-8-9860288-1-1- (HARDBACK)
LIBRARY OF CONGRESS CONTROL NUMBER:
2022914742
COVER PHOTO BY: CUEMADI WHITE AZU STUDIO
IMAGE OF FAITH FSH LLC
PO BOX 741927
RIVERDALE, GA 30274
FELICIA.HARGROVE80@GMAIL
WWW.IMAGEOFFAITHFSHLLC.COM

SPECIAL DISCOUNTS ARE AVAILABLE ON QUAN-
TITY PURCHASES BY CORPORATIONS, ASSOCIA-
TIONS, AND OTHERS.
FOR DETAILS, CONTACT THE AUTHOR AT
FELICIA.HARGROVE80@GMAIL.COM

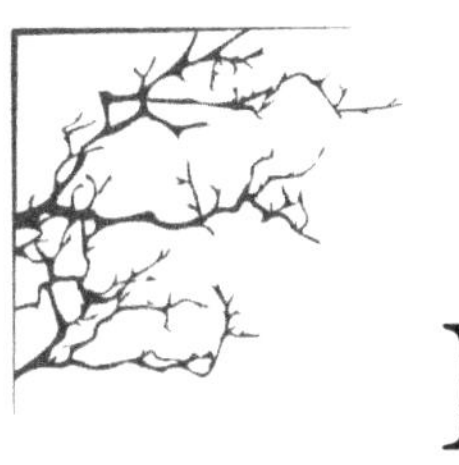

First and foremost, I would like to thank God for keeping me safe and strong through it all. I thank you my God for pushing and talking me through all my heartache, tears, and pain. YOU are the head of my life. YOU are my Savior.

I DEDICATE THIS BOOK to my grandmother The late Great Hattie "Fattie" Hargrove and my father William "Neal" Wilson who is the only father figure I have ever known. I miss you guys dearly. God rest your souls.

I give thanks to my family and friends near and far. You never doubted me, and I am very grateful.

To my small family... I dedicate this book to you. My children and husband are my everything. Jervarious, Charcell, and Faith, without you there would be no me. Thank You my love, Tarae Terrell, for dealing with my craziness. I know it has been a rollercoaster ride full of ups and downs. But see... I told you guys that it would be worth it. I LOVE YOU!!!!

ACKNOWLEDGMENTS

WRITING MY FIRST BOOK has brought back good and bad memories. However, it is worth it. It took me 20+ years to finish writing Loose Lips Sink Ships. I didn't know where to start or where to end. I finally figured it out. The time has come to share my journey with you all.

To each acknowledgment we made it. I thank each one of you for standing in my corner from beginning to end. You mean the world to me.

I love each one of you who stuck by me, encouraged me, fussed at me, and for staying with me. You pushed me to never give up. You guys are amazing. The stress was real for you and me both. Thank you for being the driving force behind this major accomplishment. WE DID IT!

Respectfully, I want to give the highest and utmost thanks to all my HATERS, all my watchers, all the ones that believed the haters, the ones that hated because they hated, the ones that hated with the haters, and all the ones that loved me but had to hate me. Thank you, HATERS! A special thank you for all the attempts to tear me down, to the ones who secretly wanted me to fail, the ones who pre-tended to be my friend, the ones who tried to turn everyone against me, the jealous ones. Some of you tried to ruin my life, my marriage, my career, and my character.

I thank you from the bottom of my heart because you pushed me to follow my dreams. You motivated me to continue my dreams and to take time for myself. It was in these moments that I became focused and ignored the distractions that were holding me back. "WHICH WAS YOU" I spent time with my family, spent time learning all about myself, and learned who was really for me. Thanks for the inspiration.

I told myself every day that anger was not the answer, and to let the dirt grow someone GREAT!! I just had to prove to you and myself that I am more than you ever thought I was. I never needed you. I still love you and I forgive you. God Bless you all and I hope you get everything you deserve in life. Thank you!!

THANK YOU, SON, *Jervarious Hargrove,* without you, there is no me. I would not have ever joined the military if I did not have the responsibility and joy of having to raise you. You made me want more out of life for us...

Thank you, son. *Charcell Hargrove,* you are my miracle child, my headache, my sweetheart, my cool dude, my son. You have tested every inch of me and kept me on my toes. You make me smile from the time I wake up until I go to bed. Thank you for my forehead kisses, my good night hugs, and my special "I love you" throughout the day.

Thank you, daughter. *Faith Rogers,* you are my planned child and my baby girl whom I wished for my entire pregnancy. Maybe I should have asked for specific instructions because you are double me. You are my twin, but you are so much smarter. I love you dearly my precious princess. You are perfect in every way.

I never knew love until I felt each one of you in my tummy. If it wasn't for you and your love, I would not have made it in this cruel world. I love you all equally!! You will never know love until you have carried a little person in your belly for nine months. I will not change motherhood for anything in the world. I love you!!!

To my husband Torrie "Tarae" Terrell thank you for being you. I thank you for being my headache and pushing me over and beyond my limits. You know I have "MANY" hats to wear, and I wear them with pride. Thank you for being patient, stern, accepting, passionate, and confident in your wife. I have learned so much from you over these nine years and I thank you for every year and every day. I love you! Family is always first!!

Special thanks to my two best friends, Anita, and Stephon. You both pushed me to write and to keep writing. You kept me on my toes on this journey called life as well as on my writing journey. You called me every other day to make sure I was not distracted. You encouraged me to write at least something every day. You held me accountable. Thank you! Thanks for your consistent friendship. We have been friends for 10+ years.

And to my new friend Suga, you know who you are. I thank you for everything and for sticking by me. You are my little firecracker.

A SPECIAL THANK YOU to my blood cousin Ulaonda. You helped me throughout my publishing process. You have been there from the day I contacted you, up until the day I finished my book. You have been there every step of the way. I am proud of you! I am proud to say that you are my writing coach, my positive energy, my confidant, my empowerment, and my family. Thanks for being a part of my writing journey. Thank you and I appreciate you from the bottom of my heart!

A special thanks to my second mother/Godmother Teresa. You have been here for me since 3rd grade. You are my savior. You came to my rescue during the toughest time in my childhood. You encouraged me to stay in school, to stay on the right path, and to stay alive. Mama Teressa, you were the one who gave me hope on this journey called life. You gave me a reason to live. You are my inspiration. You encouraged me to become the best version of myself. I love you so much for taking me under your wing. You taught me how to become a woman, to take care of myself, and you kept me from the streets. You have been my teacher. I will forever love you.

Finally, to my dear mother, I send you a BIG Thank You. Mary Burton, I thank you for giving birth to me when everyone else told you to get rid of me. Looking back, it was funny whenever you became upset you told me, "I should have ate you" Mom I'm glad you didn't eat me. Thank you for giving me a chance at life. Thank you for forcing me to become the woman I am today. You did this without knowing. You encouraged me to take charge of my life no matter what. You held me accountable for my actions. You told me that I could only blame myself for the choices I make in life. I was responsible for the life I created for myself. I will never forget these words you continuously tell me, "True love never dies tall and beautiful". I LOVE YOU, MOM!!

I thank EVERYONE who has impacted my life in any way. I love you ALL. I figured out my beginning. So, let's start here...

God my loving father, you are my confidant and my HEALER. I THANK YOU for healing and loving me. I LOVE YOU!! Here is what God has placed in my heart to share. Let the journey begin...

CHAPTER 1

The Beginning of ME

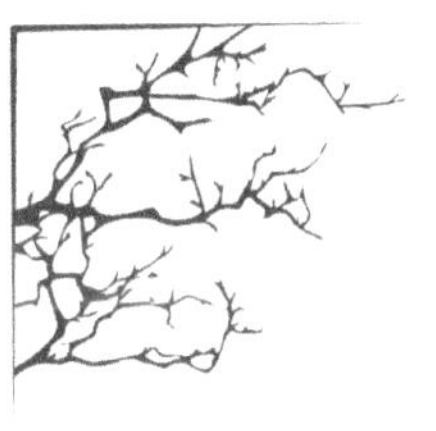

On April 23, 1980, at 11:38 pm a beautiful light red baby girl was born. Boy, did I have a head full of hair. I made my entrance at Duke Medical Center in Durham, North Carolina. My mother Martha was only 15 years old when she gave birth to me. *Oh, my goodness she was practically a baby herself.* Most of her family wanted her to abort me. Her family and the health department felt that she was too young and too small to have a baby. Martha ignored their opinions and insisted on having me anyway.

I remember the day she told me this story. I was at her house in Kinston, North Carolina where she currently resides. For whatever reason, she was angry that day, but she calmed down when she told me this story. She needed me to know that she wanted me and was going to protect me at all costs. She said "I felt you moving around in my tummy, and I wanted to have my baby" I teared up, smiled, and was overwhelmed with joy. Where I was from it was common to have babies at a young age. *I am here now; and oh, do I have a story to tell!*

I am from a small town in North Carolina called Townsville. Townsville is on the border of Virginia and is so small you will struggle to find it on the map. Those who know me today, would not believe I lived or was raised here. It does not represent my lively rich personality, but instead, you see the opposite.

I was considered a bastard child or an outsider. You see, nothing about my life history was easy. I lived with my grandmother Fattie for most of my childhood. I was happiest when I was with her. Whenever I lived with my mom I felt like an outsider, but with Fattie I felt loved. Fattie is my Big Mama. She loved me and I loved her. I am her first grandchild. Our bond was special. Fattie's complexion was dark chocolate, she had dimples, a small waist, a big butt, and moles on her face. She was very attractive and had a very nice shape. She looked too young to be anyone's grandma.

Fattie didn't speak much. However, whenever she did speak, she spoke wisdom to me and her family. She said to me before I went to school, "Do not let no one take your stuff, do not let no one touch your hair, and do not let anyone bully you. She always told me to be careful. She kissed my forehead every day and said to me "you are so pretty Lee Lee" She took care of me. She was my protector. She took me away from the incest that was going on with the family and all the *cousins make dozen and kin make twins bullshit*. She did not leave me alone with anyone in her apartment, not even her sons. No matter how bad she wanted to, there was no way she could protect me every second.

Fattie was always cooking and singing. She was a beast in the kitchen. I visualize her with a Newport cigarette hanging off her lip. *Boy, do I miss her!* I remember her teaching me how to cook. I stayed in the kitchen with her. She had me cooking at eight. She taught me how to cook and season the meat. She taught me how to bake pies and cakes. If you know me today, you now know why I love to cook. Baking is what I remember the most. Oh my, I can just smell the room. Blackberry cobbler, fried potatoes, strawberry shortcake, dumplings, and cakes. She cooked all those sweets just for me. I believe this was her way of showing me how much she loved me. It worked; sweets and spending time with her made me happy.

It seemed as if I was with Fattie everywhere she went. Sadly, I was there with her during her hospital stay when she was fighting cancer. I was there with her when she lost her right breast, then the left breast. Although she was very sick, she put me on the bus for school every morning. She also waited for me every day to get off. I loved every minute of it. I felt the love from her every being. I admired her strength, but I HATED cancer!!!

My Big Mama was ill, and I knew it. I could tell when she started losing weight. She started to be weak day by day. She did not want me to worry at all, but I could see cancer eating her away. It started with her breasts. She had to have both of them cut off. Cancer then spread through her body. She was becoming weaker and weaker by the day. Fattie was sick. It started to take over each organ in her body.

My grandmother cried for me to stay with her. She cried because she knew what would happen if I went to live in Townsville with my mother. She was just as much attached to me as I was to her. My grandmother must have felt like I felt. She knew I was safe with her. I felt safe with her!! She was the most important person to me. Every time you saw Fattie you saw Lee Lee. Then one day unexpectedly she was taken away from me. *I was devastated. I was numb. I couldn't even cry..*

I couldn't even feel the pain when she passed away. The pain was so deep and lingering that I could not feel anything. I knew life was about to be hard for me from that day on. I was completely numb. I knew no one else would love me as she did, cook for me like she did, or take care of me as she did.

Guess where I have to go now? Yes, back to being the outsider, the half-sister, the bastard child, the nobody.

I knew that mom loved me, but it was not the same love shown to me as it was to her other children. I became used to it at some point. Nothing mattered.

Now let me introduce you to my mother Martha. She is so beautiful, and her smile can light up a room. She was 5ft. 5in tall, had small dimples in the corner of her cheeks, brown skin, and a very nice shape. She had a bad body; especially after having four kids. It seemed like everyone was after her. She wore her hair in a long jerry curl most of the time. You still could see the pain in her beautiful brown eyes. You could tell that she had some struggles in her life. It was easy to tell that she had been through some things, some challenges, and some fears. Where we were from almost everyone had been molested, fondled, or touched. No one seemed to be exempt.

One thing about mom was that she did not take any shit from NOBODY! She fought girls and boys if needed. For a long time, people around her called her *he-man* because they said she was strong as an ox.

My mom was mean when she wanted to be and nice when she felt like it. *I mean who doesn't feel this way right?* She's my mother and I love her no matter what. Sometimes she put her hand over my mouth and nose until I passed out. She also bit my face. Sometimes she laughed as if it was funny and other times it was meant as a punishment. I didn't like it.

I remember one day my siblings and I were at home; we must've done something bad. She got a switch from a tree outside. She was ready to whip us all, but I told her I would take the whipping. My sisters were too small. I hated seeing them get whipped. She said, "oh so you a badass; you go take the whippings for everyone." She beat the crap out of me with that tree branch. *OUCH!!* I had welts all over my body. I could barely lay down.

Mom was sweet sometimes too. She let us ride to Food Lion with her. She let us pick our favorite snacks. We chose pickles, chips, and pickled pig's feet. She allowed me to hang out with my God Mom often. She would throw me birthday parties and I enjoyed them. Overall, Mom had a very good soul. She had a determined attitude. When she *wants what she wants, she gets it*. I think I get this from her. When she wasn't happy no one around her would be either. Meaning if ANYONE pissed her off; EVERYONE would have a bad day. She mostly fussed and made us clean up the entire house.

But guess what? I still loved her like no other. But the thing was, I never felt that my mother loved me. I never felt it. I don't remember her hugging me or hearing her say "I love you."

I have two sisters Tiesha and Elana and one brother Willy. I felt all the attention went to them. I would see Mom give them hugs and kisses. She gave them food stamps to go to the store. They were able to go outside to play. The fun stuff. I had to clean, cook, do my sister's hair, and get everyone ready for school. When they had nightmares, they could go lay with her in bed. *Not Me!* If I tried to do that I would get yelled at. I felt like an outsider, and I felt this way for most of my childhood.

My brother Willy and I are months close in age. I was born in April, and she was pregnant in October with him. Willy was the joking type. He picked on me and my sisters every single day. He didn't stop until he made us cry and he laughed. It seemed as if it made him happy to see us upset or crying. He called me big nose, called Elana hot tamale or big red, and called Tiesha burger or spit toes. Now that I think about it, he was funny. Willy had seizures so he got away with a lot. I often wished I was strong enough to beat him up.

My sisters were always under me. I was the one who mostly cared for them. They were just normal kids. They both are high yellow and beautiful. But they had their daddy texture of hair which was thick and nappy. They hated when I did their hair for school. Three ponytails were enough for me. I was their protector. I was to them what Fattie was to me. Tiesha and Elana held my hand as we skipped to the bus stop. Willy didn't seem to care about me walking with him. If he did, he didn't show it. They all were my heart.

I had a great relationship with my sisters, especially Tiesha. But Willy and I didn't speak much. One day, I had to fight another boy for him because he was scared. A neighborhood bully named

Romel was trying to fight Willy and somehow Romel and I ended up fighting. I only won because his arms got caught up in his shirt. *Don't mess with us!!* I've always been about protecting my family.

I have no clue who my real father is. I heard Mom and Nate talk about John, but I've never seen him. I only heard stories about him having a bunch of children and how he worked for the phone company. Other than that, I didn't know who the hell he was and didn't care. I knew that Nate was not my father. As a child, I felt he loved me differently than he loved his other kids. It is hard to describe, but I knew the love was not the same. *Ok now that you know a little history about my family; let me share my life story with you.*

CHAPTER 2

Back to Square ONE

A few weeks had passed, and Mom had me stay overnight at her best friend Jessica's house. She wanted to party. Nate, my stepdad, owned a club. I called it a little hole in the wall. It was called Nate's, and everyone in that area seemed to love it. Whenever the club was opened, there were cars parked all up and down the road. I guess it was because there was nowhere else for them to go. The nearest grocery store was more than 20 miles away. There were only small country stores there and they kept the basic needs.

Oh no. My life is ready to get worse. Talk about childhood trauma!!

I had a bad feeling, and I knew my life was going to change. Mom left me at that house alone with a teenage girl. Her name was Shan and she was 14 or 15. I was only eight. She and Nate felt it was a good idea to leave us alone for them to go party. Well, it *WAS NOT!!! Guess what she did to me?* She *MOLESTED* me, and made me lick on her vagina. She also made me touch her breast and vagina. She did the same to me. She hurt me once by using her fingers or objects. I didn't know if it was right or wrong. I just went with the flow. I only knew that I could not tell anyone. *Oh, it gets worse!* Mom sent me there every time they went to a party. *Yes, I was molested every single time.* Sadly, for me, it began to feel as if it was normal and ok. Oh, how I wish I could hug my little self and tell me

"No, Lee Lee this is not normal. This is rape and it is a crime!!!"

About a year later we moved to Henderson, North Carolina. We moved to a trailer park named Spain. Things seem to be normal for a while. Some of my cousins lived there and we would do kid stuff. We walked to the bus stop, walked to the store, rode bikes, rode skates, climbed trees, and played in the dirt. The kid stuff: I felt like a kid. Life seemed normal. I was not popular at all. I did not have the best clothes or shoes. I thought to myself; at *least I have clothes and shoes.*

I went to a school named L.B. Yancey Elementary. I was in the third grade when I started there. I was bullied throughout elementary school. I sat alone. The cafeteria lady Tessa noticed. Tessa was a tall dark skin lady with a big smile. But she didn't smile all the time. We could tell she had some spunk in her. She was tall for a woman and always had a fade boy haircut. She had a lot of earrings in her ear from the top to the bottom. She loved kids. She spent time with all the bad ones in my class. If you made her mad, we all knew it because she went off. There were a lot of bad kids there, a lot!

Tessa was nice to me. She took quite an interest in me. Every day at lunch she gave me free stuff. All the things I could not buy such as pickles, cookies, and sometimes cake. I think she knew I was having some issues at home. Tessa took me under her wing. One day I was in the cafeteria sucking my thumb. (a habit and soothing technique that I did until I was twenty-one) I was being teased about my hair. I guess she felt bad for me because she gave me a cookie and a pickle. She said, "here you go, pretty girl." Whenever she sees me, she still calls me "pretty girl". I was happy to have someone to show me, love.

I loved school more than I loved being home except for the bullying part. I loved learning, the activities, and the teachers. The teachers were so nice to me. I loved lunch. I loved seeing Tessa. I loved school, but my grades did not reflect this. My grades were not good enough. I failed the third grade for some reason. I'm guessing it was from being moved around or maybe it was from all the trauma that I was experiencing at home. I could not fully focus on my schoolwork.

One day, I was home with my mom Martha, her sister Elsa, her best friend Pat, Nat's sister, Dot, and some other people. They were drinking and having a good time. I was not old enough to fully understand what was happening, but I was old enough to know that some shit was going down. *Just let me say my mother was a beast and no one wanted to fuck with her when she got mad.* All I knew was that a whole fight broke out. Mom jumped on her best friend Pat. She jumped on my stepdad too, oh she went crazy. My mouth dropped. I was shocked and scared. I hid behind the couch. I saw things and knives being thrown. I saw my mom crying and everybody running for cover. My mom beat her ass and Pat got the fuck up out of there.

From my understanding, this happened because she found out my stepdad Nat had been sleeping with her best friend Pat. Pat swore that it didn't happen. Seemed that everyone knew but my mom. She was not playing at all. She divorced him as soon as possible. Now, this was when shit hit the fan for me. My life became more complicated, and life was ready to take a turn for the worse. My mom was so strong-headed; she didn't think before she did things. I guess this is the beginning of me becoming who I am.

We moved to Hillcrest Apartments. The projects and the low-key hood. I made it to the fifth grade making good grades. I did so well that they moved me up a grade. Tessa was still in contact with me. Some of my family lived in Hillcrest. My aunt Elsa lived up the street with her three children and my cousin stayed next door to us. My granddad, his girlfriend, and her daughter lived there. I was confused about the whole situation, so I never asked any questions. But I learned that my grandfather eventually had a baby with his wife's daughter and yes, I said it right; but that was nothing new because that shit happened all the time. He also had children with two sisters. This shit seemed normal.

I was now comfortable and thought things were getting better. Not!! My aunt Trina was a hoe, and everyone knew it she was fucking whoever she wanted. She had a car, partied a lot, and seemed to be having so much fun. Trina being a hoe was a bad thing for me because people thought we all were hoes. She lived back and forth from our house to Elsa. I mean who knew where she stayed? It hurt my feelings when people talked about my Aunt Trina. I loved her and she was like an older friend to me. Trina had a nice coke bottle shape. It seemed as if everybody wanted her. Rumors said everybody had her. She kept herself looking nice. Her hair was done nicely. She was well known everywhere in Henderson.

I was 12 and I babysat and cooked for my family's children. I was the babysitter and boy was I pissed. Mom was too busy running behind men. She started dating Luther and he was a fat bald mean man. He lived almost an hour away and she would haul ass down there whenever he called. We all slept in one room just so she could be with him. *He looked fat and nasty. What did she see in this man? He had a gold tooth for Christ's sake.* I didn't see what she saw in him. She was head over heels for him.

Things were so bad that I tried to commit suicide. I was only 12. I tried to cut my wrist with a razor blade when I was home. I just felt overwhelmed and frustrated. I saw a therapist about my issues with depression. I think I never got over the fact that my grandmother passed. I knew I would never be loved as she loved me. No one would pay attention to me as she did. I missed her and I took it harder than I thought. My mind was rambling 100 miles an hour.

I thought Luther was beating Mom. I never physically saw him hit her, but I heard him yell and throw shit a lot. He did not like when she brought us there. After a while, she left us home alone and went to see him.

I had to take on the adult responsibilities at this time for my siblings. I became the parent of Tiesha, Elana, and Willy. It didn't bother me at first but after a while it became overwhelming. Oh, and by the way, we have not seen my stepdad, Nate, since the fight. We heard he married some ugly cross-eyed lady with five kids. Martha and Luther broke up. The break-up sent her into a frenzy. I had never seen her smoke until then. She started smoking weed like a choo choo train. It calmed her down and relaxed her I guess . *Oh, it gets worse y'all. Stay with me.*

I was at Eaton Johnson Middle School and one-day multiple kids came up to me in the hallway. They told me they saw my mom beat some lady's ass at the carwash. OMG!! I was embarrassed but I'm glad she didn't get beat up. A few weeks later the bitch she beat up came to our house with a little 22 gun. Yikes! My mom told us calmly to get back in the house. She told the heffa "if you gonna do it go ahead and do it." Wow, I told you my mom was a beast. They were fighting over Luther's fat ass. So many things happened quickly; so, keep up with me. When I got to school the next day, they still were talking about that shit. We ended up moving to Raleigh, North Carolina. and guess what now? WE ARE HOME-LESS! Things didn't go as planned. We were supposed to move in with Uncle Ralph.

I was mad and tired of moving. Mom was running from a man, and we all suffered because of it. We slept in our car and lived in shelters. There were sixty beds in one room. *I HATED IT!* We deserved so much better. We were poor!! I saw my first dead body by this shelter. My mom worked at a hotel near there for a little while. We hid inside the hotel and helped her clean the rooms. I learned how to do the fucking hotel crease for the beds. A few months later we ended up back in Henderson, North Carolina. My mom started dating this nigga named Bob. She also dated a few police officers and some well-known young guys from the neighborhood. She was private about who she dated or fucked. She denied anyone who said they messed around. However, when she was in a relationship with someone, she was ALL for that person.

At the age of 13, I did a stupid thing for attention. I took a nude picture and it got out everywhere at school and in the neighborhood. I was embarrassed and hurt. I showed it to someone who I thought I could trust. Van ran off with it and I never saw it again. After all the backlash I felt worthless and just wanted to end it all. I tried to commit suicide again. I knew I did not want to feel the same pain from the first attempt so I thought pills would be easier. I took a bunch of pills. The pills only made me sleep a few hours and I woke up. I was upset that it did not work at all. My mom didn't find out for three months. There was no support. I just had to suffer the consequences. I was sad and embarrassed at the same time, but I dealt with it well.

Well, Bob beat her ass almost every day and did not care if we were around. We didn't understand why he beat her. I was a confused little girl. One day he beat her ass so badly; that she went into the closet and pulled out her shotgun. She shot at his ass. She had enough! Well, that was the last time he put his hands on her. He got the fuck up out of that house. We never heard from his old red ass again. I was drained at this point and was not feeling this. I knew that no man would put their hands on me ever. My mom told us, girls, "NEVER let a man beat on you cause I've taken all the ass whippings for y'all"

CHAPTER 3

A Teenager Crying for Attention

I started liking boys and having sex at 14. I was curious. I had sex with the cutest guy in my school. He was from New York and his name was Rolin. He was tall with long braids. His complexion was tan, and he was very sexy. *Guess what he did?* Yep...He went to school the next day and told everyone. This was when I lost trust in boys. I learned that boys or men just want one thing. I never saw him again. I heard that he is currently in prison for something big. I also learned if a boy cared for you, he would wait until you are ready. I almost had sex with the boy across the street, but I got scared when I saw his dick. His dick was way too big for me. I changed my mind quickly.

I began to act like a typical teenager. I was smelling myself around this age. I didn't care about anything or anyone. I had no stability in my life. I started exploring and was hot in the ass. I hung out with this older girl named Tomika from up the street. She lived in the K building, and we lived in the A building. Tomika was nice to me, and she seemed to be my friend. But I think she was the one bringing girls for her brother. I attracted the older crowd because I was not popular with kids my age. Well at a young age I started to have sex with Tomika brother James who was much older than I was. He was nearly ten years older than me. *What was I thinking???*

James was tall and had a big nose. He was not attractive at all, but I was craving attention from anyone. He met my needs at that time. He gave me the attention I wanted, needed, and craved. I didn't care about our age gap. I wanted to be wanted. I found out his ungrateful ass was fucking with someone else. So, I had sex with his friend Tommy. I did not need that type of attention. He was too old for me and a little girl like me was just a fuck. He knew he could work my mind and get what he wanted which was sex. He took advantage of me. James and I never contacted one another again. I saw him at the club called the Barn but would not give him the time of day when he flirted. I had moved on. I was proud of myself for staying in school and caring for my siblings. Cooking for them and making sure they got on the school bus was a must.

My aunt Trina dated this guy named Black. His name was so weird to me because he was red. I hung out with my aunt often and I met a lot of new people. I met this boy named Riley. He was my age. I wanted someone to kick it with. We kicked it for a little while. Mom was comfortable with him. He came over to our apartment one day and we had sex. Mom was there and we did not care! She did not either!! She didn't say shit because she was in the room probably doing the same thing with the young dude from the neighborhood. I was shocked that she even fucked him.

After a while, I did not fuck with Riley anymore. I was not sure why we stopped talking but we did. I started dating a guy named Caine. Caine had a dark chocolate complexion and a very low haircut. He was nice and I enjoyed his company. He walked on his tippy toes and seemed feminine but of course, he liked girls. He liked me. Oh, and he did have a car which was good for me. I was 15 and he was 17. Age was not a factor back in the 90s. We did not care about age nor did ANY guy in Henderson, North Carolina. The song by Aaliyah, *Age Ain't Nothing but a Number* was popping. It seems like all the old ass men wanted to fuck the young girls.

Caine and I had sex a lot. He had a nice size dick that I enjoyed. I sneaked him through the window when I knew my mom was high as hell or when she was asleep. I was learning and living life right now. Now that I think about it, I was not living life. I was being hot in the ass and stupid. Caine picked me up in his little red car. I never had anyone drive me around, so I felt like he liked me. *He loved himself some Fee.* I liked Caine but I was a kid myself. I was young and confused. I had no clue what I wanted out of life. I did not know who I wanted to be or where I wanted to go. Honestly, I don't even know if I want to finish school. So, having a boyfriend was the least of my concerns.

I was young and only wanted to have fun. I remember chatting on the phone with this dude from school that I wanted to get to know named Que. *Yes, I dated a lot of boys. I didn't have sex with all of them though. I told you I was exploring and was hot in the ass.* Que was tall and wore big glasses, but he was nice and goofy to me. We met in ROTC classes. I invited him to my birthday party. He said he was coming. I was excited. Suddenly I heard a strange voice, and his uncle Tony B was on the phone. He was talking crazy and asked to get with me. He said he wanted to have sex and called me beautiful. *What is wrong with this man?* He said he was in his thirties. I told him he was too old for me and was old enough to date my mother. Of course, he said the most popular line of the 90's "age ain't nothing but a number." He continued begging. I told him "Hell no" and that he could kick it with my mother. NOW, THIS WOULD BECOME TO BE THE BIGGEST MISTAKE I HAVE EVER MADE IN MY LIFE. I had a birthday party in April 1996 and a few of my friends came over to celebrate my sweet 16. Tony B came with Que to my party and Mom and Tony B hit it off. He was a curse! He had my mom's head gone all the way.

The pain that I felt bled my heart so bad. I just could not shake this feeling of abandonment and rejection from Mom. She gave the love that I wanted and needed from her to men. *MEN seemed to be the most important thing in her life.* But I saw her giving Tony B everything and her mind was gone about him. No matter what he did or what we told her she would never listen to us. She made me feel as if we were just nagging children or should I say I was a nagging teenager. *I just knew that there was something up with him.* Someone even told me he was having sex with a 16-year-old at the time. Of course, he denied it.

I took a bottle of Zoloft and tried to end my life. I did not want to live anymore. The pain I was feeling was just too much for me. I was hurt mentally, physically, and emotionally. My feelings were hurt, and I didn't know what to do. My life seemed like the walls were closing in on me. I told myself, If I take these pills all my pain will stop. This will be easy; I will just go to sleep and never wake up again. That's exactly what I wanted. I took thirty pills with milk that day and called my aunt Glen afterward. I said to her, "I love you. I will never see you again" She tried to keep me on the phone, but I hung up. She lived far away, and my thought process was that she would not get there in time to save me.

I woke up in the hospital. I saw doctors and nurses standing over me. They were pumping my stomach. I didn't know what was going on. I saw a familiar face. I saw Mom and I heard her say "she will be ok." *Can you believe this woman! SHE DIDN'T EVEN CARE that I tried to take my 'life. She was still looking for Tony B.* After this, shit changed for me. I started thinking of myself. The social worker that came to check on me asked me if I wanted to go home and I told her *NO*. She asked if I wanted to be committed and I said *YES!* I was sent to a mental institution for 90 days. My cousin, my current boyfriend Caine, and his sister Shonda visited me there. I do not remember my mother visiting me at all.

It was time for me to leave the hospital and go home. I didn't want to go home. I ate a lot of good food and met new people while I was there. I was prepared for the bullshit at home because I knew nothing had changed. Things seemed worse and I was on a road to destruction. Then one day, Mom and Tony B got into an argument. Tony B wrote on my mom's mirror I love you Boobie #1 and I wrote I DON'T. They had nicknames for one another *Boobie1 was my mom's nickname* and *Boobie2 was Tony B's nickname*. Boy did my mom flip bricks when she saw that I wrote "I don't love you" and she thought Tony B wrote it. At this age, I did not know why I did it. But I was saying to her that I *didn't love her*. Once she learned that I wrote it she went crazy. She flipped the TV over and yelled in my face; "I am never leaving Tony B, and if you don't like it, then leave." I didn't think she would get this upset with me.

I remember this day so clearly because it was snowing badly. She was pissed and I said nothing. She cared about only him. I was crying for attention. I later told her that she didn't show us any love and that we needed her. She got mad and said "y'all don't need me. I need

Tony B." I was over this, and I turned to the streets for love. I left. I left home in the snow and walked to my aunt April's house. I cried all the way there. I was unable to concentrate. Before I left, I stole a bunch of weed out of her closet. She didn't think I knew where it was hidden. It was in the attic. I knew a lot. I kept quiet. I also knew that her new Lil New York boyfriend, Tony B had talked her into selling dope out of the house. They mailed it to the empty house next door to us. I don't even know why I stole it because I didn't even smoke. But I tried it that day. *No worries, I hated it. Mary Jane is not for me.* It made me so high, and I never touched it again.

We moved back to Raleigh. Yep! You guessed it. I was 16. Mom was on the run again. She was running away from her problems. She and Tony B had gotten into some shit, and she was pissed about it. Tony B never said what was wrong. But I do know the police came to search our house for drugs. I don't remember why we were running again but we were running. She faked being homeless to get help another way. I got my first job at Checkers because I wanted to help. That didn't last long. We moved into a very small house.

Our aunt Trina moved to Raleigh to help us out. She watched us. It worked out for her as well because she was having some issues back in Henderson. I guess my mom did not resolve whatever she and Tony B had going on because we did not see him for a while. That was short-lived. There was a bad storm/tornado coming our way. Mom left before we could take shelter. She went looking for her Boobie2. She left our ass in the house in the middle of the storm. Trina was with us during this all. The lights went out and a tree fell on our house.

Oh my, we were so terrified and did not know what to do. We called and called Mom. We did not know what to do. Then she appeared a few days later as if nothing happened. She did not seem to care that we were in danger a few days ago. Instead, she talked about moving to Kinston. Kinston is where Tony B and his mother lived. I learned from the past that there was no need to express our feelings. I did not talk or fuss. I kept my feelings to myself. She did what she wanted to do no matter what. I assumed they were back on good terms again.

We moved to Kinston, North Carolina about two months later. Oh, by the way, I dropped out of school right before we moved to Kinston. There was so much going on in my life. I hung out with the popular kids and dated a popular basketball player named Squad. I played basketball, I ran track, I played softball, and I was in ROTC. My home life was so stressful that I dropped out of school. I was totally broken and could not concentrate on school. My mind was all over the place. I still had people bullying me, I carried canned goods to school in my bookbag. This was my protection. This was how I was going to defend myself. I hated school even though I loved my teachers and wanted to learn. I hated that I had to be someone that I did not want to be to have friends.

Tony B's mom lived in Kinston, and we followed him. I lived there for a few months, but I just could not stay. I did not think my mom would ever change. She was all about protecting him, not her children. I had to go. I moved back to Henderson, my hometown. I went back to living the way I wanted to. Reckless. All I wanted was to be loved. I did not care about anything anymore. I got drunk, partied, fucked, and cried A LOT. I was a wreck.

I started dating Main. He was a popular drug dealer. He was about 6ft 6in and weighed about 350lbs or more. He was a gentle giant. He was nice. I thought that he had money because he had a nice car with loud music. That was the thing back in the day. Let me tell you how we met. It all started when I was at my cousin's Pepper house and my friend with the same name as I started hanging out a lot. I was just going from house to house living and sleeping where I could. *Who am I kidding?* I was low-key homeless, but I kept my clothes at my aunt April's house.

Main came over to Pepper's house one day, and there was a bet about us fucking. He ordered us whatever pizza we wanted. I guess Pepper and Freda said we were scared. I was really scared, to be honest. We joked around and said we would pretend that we did. We were digging one another, and it happened anyway. We fucked. It was crazy but it was fun at the same time. Well, long story short me and Main started dating. We had a lot in common. We shared the same birthday, we liked motorcycles, and we wanted something out of life. We were in love! So, I thought.

I thought he was different. *HE WAS NOT!* I later found out he had a whole family and a baby on the way. I was so hurt!! BUT we kept dating. I did not believe the rumors. I found out later that he was having sex with one of my cousins Joan. Joan and I were not close. I didn't even know her like that. I just knew we were cousins down the line, maybe third or fourth cousins. I thought she was a man when I first saw her. She was at least six feet tall, with dark skin, a small nose, a nice shape, and small lips. She was not the finest. It had to be the pussy because it was not the looks. I was hurt! *How could he do this to me?* I thought he loved me.

I called him the night before and all day that day. He ignored my calls. I heard from the grapevine where to find him. I drove by her house at four a.m. in the morning and YES! He was there. That was the day I left and went back to Kinston with my mom. I wanted to try again. I felt that I needed to go and keep an eye on my sisters and try to graduate from high school. That was the least I could do.

Now that you know a little about me, let's get to the juicy part! Time to loosen these lips!!

CHAPTER 4

Learning Lessons

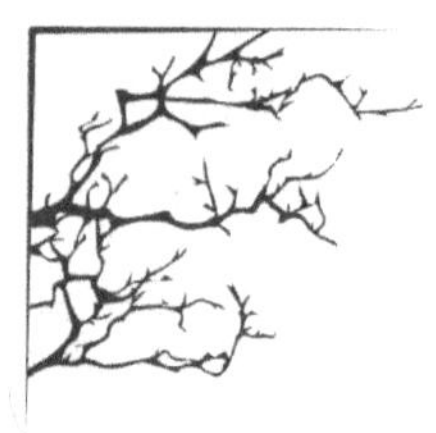

I was quiet, shy, and the person who didn't react to anything said or done to me. I allowed anger to build up and then I blew up when I couldn't handle it anymore. Fast forward to today, my writing is a form of me blowing up differently. I feel that writing this book will stop a lot of talking and clear a whole lot of rumors. Maybe it will clear up some of the gossip, hearsay, comments, assumptions, drama, talk, tittle-tattle, the word on the street, allegedly, or I heard that happened. So, pull up a chair and get ready for the *Tea*. There have been a few people in my inbox asking me, "Did this really happen? I heard you did this, and you are at fault for this/that." I heard several stories and of course, I was the villain in them. I know the truth!!!

I proudly do not care, and therefore it is time to share my story with you. It has been 20+ years and I have never had the desire of clearing anything up or telling my truth until now. When I heard lie after lie repeatedly it set fuel to my soul. Now that my children are grown and understand right from wrong, I'm ready. *Do you want to know what happened?* I will tell you my story and we all know that there are several sides to a story. Their side (what usually makes them look good) My side (which is my truth) People's assumptions and the TRUTH (Only God knows the truth!!!)

So, who can tell my story better than I can? NOT A FUCKING SOUL other than ME!! I am no angel by far, but I do not treat innocent people like shit. This means I do not go around intentionally hurting people or fucking with folk with the intent of harm. I have been quiet for years and allowed people to drag my name through the mud. *NOT ANYMORE!* I am done with saving everyone else's name and face. I will no longer let humans, people, opportunists, individuals, and narcissists destroy my character. Some people just want to hold on to their lies; Just so they can look good. They want to be the hero. THEY PRETEND TO BE THE VICTIM or maybe they want their wives to stay blind to the truth. It is easier to have me look like the evil villain, the home wrecker, the hoe, etc. You know I could be an evil villain if I wanted to be. I put all my fears in a basket and decided it was time to clear a lot of things up on my end.

You see 20 years ago, some things happened that I am not proud of. I will take the blame for everything that I have done. You will learn of these as you journey with me as I share. My intention is not to hurt anyone's feelings, but I don't care if it does. I just want you all to know my truth and how this really went down. The air needs to be cleared at this point. As you journey with me today, I want you to know that *I love my life and I love my children. Nothing or no one will ever change that.*

I admit I have flaws and I have my funny ways. I can be very revengeful when I'm hurting. I get angry quickly. Sometimes out of anger I say things I do not mean or maybe I hold my anger in too long and say the wrong things. I drink a lot when I'm upset. I cheat if you cheat recklessly, I lack confidence, too nice, and I don't like being wrong. Yes, I have A LOT of flaws, but I accept myself. My delivery sometimes comes off harsh and I am learning to control that. I HATE being accused of something that I did not do or cause. A good example of what I am saying is:

You can't accidentally fall on a niggas dick without an agreement or their participation.

I am as real as they come. I don't switch up. I am the person you can talk to and trust with your secrets. I have learned so many lessons over the years and I do not regret anything that has happened. I would not be where I am today if I did not endure the lessons. There is so much to talk about when it comes to me. The beginning is tragic, the middle is extremely interesting, and the end is still going. I can't tell the whole story right now, but let's continue...So let's spill some real tea.

I went back to school in 1997 and worked toward my high school diploma. Mom and I began to have a relationship again. She drove and picked me up from school. She had turned her life around and started going to church. WOW! She did an entire 360. She was a church-going Christian lady. We went to bible study every Wednesday night, church all day Sunday, and whenever the pastor wanted his two disciples to come to the church. We had to go as well.

Mom and Tony B got married in the spring of 1997. They were heavy in the church so they kind of had to get married. The pastor said you "can't be shacking up." At some point, she stopped the church stuff and went back to the drug stuff. Her husband was a fake to me and a pervert. One day I caught Tony B in my sister's bedroom looking under the blanket as they slept. My sisters were 11 and 13. I screamed, WHAT THE FUCK ARE YOU DOING? He looked startled just like he saw a ghost. He said, I was covering them up. I said, "No you weren't." Mom came out the room and she asked what was going on. I told her what happened, and she blew it off. I said Fuck it. She would never see him as the pervert that he was and probably will always be. I dealt with him because I had to. I was going to be the one to protect my sisters.

Tony B introduced me to an older man named KT. He is Tony B's cousin. I was 17 and he was 33. He would come by a lot, and I never knew why. My stepfather said to me "he likes you and you should kick it with him." My mom was fine with it because they needed drugs and he was a drug dealer. It seemed as if I was a trade-off. I ended up falling in love with him. Later he told me I was his drug dealer. I didn't understand. I do now. They both wanted me to be friendly with him for their personal needs. Well, their plan worked because KT became my boo thang. My boo thang got caught and went to prison. He left me. KT was taking good care of me until then.

I thought for a long time that he was going to get out. He wrote letters to me often. He had me all hyped up about him getting out. He talked about us being together and he loved me. He had me doing weird things like writing a passage from the bible. Then he would ask me to curse out whoever put him there. I had to continuously write the passage over and over with the district's attorney name on it. Weird right? Yeah, I was fooling myself. I was a young dummy. I was 18 years old and still lost. I learned so much and lost so much. Yes, I was older, but I still had not learned anything. *I HAVE NOTHING!* I have no high school diploma, no car, no money, no love, and no career. *Oh, and guess what?* Yeah, I just found out that I was pregnant. I felt like a failure. I had failed myself and my unborn child. I had dreams of being somebody and having a great life. I wanted to be successful. I decided to make a change for us; My baby and me.

I guess drugs started having Mom lose focus because she started forgetting to pick me up from school. I started walking five miles to and from school. I was pregnant and determined to be successful. I was five months pregnant when I found out I was pregnant. I went to the doctor to receive my next dose of depo shot and found out I was pregnant. *How did I get pregnant on the depo shot.?* I guess I was part of the 1%. Some days I cried to school and some days I sang to school. I made it through school pregnant and all while walking. I walked to and from Lenoir Community College to get my High School Diploma. I DID IT Y'ALL! I received my high school diploma in July 1998. I was so proud of myself. I felt in my heart on that day that I could accomplish anything. I knew I was stronger than I thought.

I told myself, *If I could survive my childhood, I can survive anything.*

I know the question is *where's your baby daddy? Ok, Well here's the scoop.* I was not trying to get pregnant in the first place. I was hot in the ass and shit happened. I met Trey at Lenoir Community College when I was going to school to get my diploma. We were just having fun and the condom broke. Trey was a nice guy and kind of goofy. He was about 5ft 11in. tall. He was dark-skinned, slim, muscular, and had pointy ears. I think he was African. I was attracted mostly to his personality. Trey liked me and he wanted to be with me. We could have had the perfect little family, but that's not what

I wanted. I didn't know him like that. Besides, a relationship was not what I wanted. I was young and confused about life. Trey stuck around for a little while. It seemed as if he was pretending to care and pretending to want to be in our child's life. He begged for sex more than he bought for our child. He was unattractive to me, and his dick was a little too big for me anyway, *I loved my walls.*

Everything changed quickly. Trey got himself a girlfriend and now suddenly our baby isn't his. He said it was Main's baby. I had broken up with Main months ago. *Y'all do remember Main, right? He was the guy who cheated on me with cousin. Yeah, the loser.* I learned a long time ago that Main couldn't have babies, so he said and as much as we fucked, I never got pregnant by him. I knew who my baby daddy was and that's that. You see I wrote a lot back then just as much as I write now. I kept records. I had a calendar, journal, and notebook, and I wrote everything in there. I wrote my period dates, days I had sex, and with who. So, I knew. I know the timelines were close, but I kept tabs on myself and my pussy.

I was proud of myself. I just received my diploma, and this was a big accomplishment. I wanted something out of life for myself. I wanted to do it for myself and not ask anyone for shit. I still didn't feel accomplished though. I researched classes that were offered at the community college. I wanted to find something that caught my eye. I wanted to do something I liked or loved. I went to accounting classes for three months and I *QUIT! That stuff was hard.* However, I did learn to type. I can now type 75 words a minute if not more. I also practiced over the years of course. Yes! I found something I liked. I took a nail tech class and I enjoyed it. I graduated from my nail tech class in October 1998; It only took about three months. Now, this was the time I anticipated.

I was good at what I did, and it made me smile. I felt like I was getting somewhere. After I graduated from nail school my teacher opened a nail shop. She was excited for us. She recruited me and everyone who was in my graduating class that year. This was perfect timing because the responsibility will soon be different from me just taking care of myself. I will soon have a baby boy. Now it was the time that I had been anticipating. The birth of my son. Jervarious Hargrove aka Dontay is my pride and joy. I had my son in November 1998. He was so handsome! He had dark chocolate smooth skin. I love him so much. He had beautiful round dark brown eyes, dimples, and a head full of charcoal black hair. I had a beautiful real-life baby doll.

I was a new teenage mom. It was now time for me to put on my big girl panties. I was approved for a section 8 apartment. My rent was only fifty dollars. I was getting an SSI check, so I had no problem with that. I was so happy to have my apartment. I received help from a social worker named Sandy. I met her at the clinic where my OBGYN doctor was. She worked there. She was an older white lady with dark hair. It looked like she dyed her hair a lot from the way her roots looked. She was extremely nice, and she wanted to help me. She knew I needed help and she cared enough to help me. She saw me walk there to get my prenatal care. I bet she felt sorry for me. In conversation, I did tell her I walked everywhere I needed to go.

I still felt unaccomplished. I wanted more. *Look at me...* I have no car, I am on food stamps, on section 8, and my credit score sucked. I felt alone. I felt like I didn't have any guidance. My mother had nothing going for herself. No one in my family had anything or worked towards having anything. There seemed to be no good influences in the family. All I knew at that moment was that I didn't want to live like everyone else. I want something out of life. *SOME-THING*!! I was hard on myself. I asked myself, *now what the fuck do I suppose to do, and where am I going from here?* I wanted to pay my little bills on time. I didn't know how important a credit score was. However, I knew I wanted a good score. Having my spot was a big accomplishment. I can say I was proud of that. I was so happy. I did not have to listen to Mom, or I did not have to sleep on the porch whenever I was ten minutes late from the curfew. Yes. I slept on the porch a time or two.

I was happy as fuck now. I was living recklessly. Mom babysat my son for me all the time. I started hanging out with the wrong crowd. I invited a lot of friends over and we partied. I spent my food stamps on cookouts. I was a drinker. I drank a lot when I was in a party mood. My friend Sid the barber used to buy it for me because I was underage. Sid was my best friend at the time. I thought Sid was gay. I later found out he was not because he screwed my cousin. She was in town visiting me. It did not bother me because I was not interested in him like that. I saw him as a friend. Sid and I hung out all the time and he loved my son Donny. He kept his hair fresh all the time. It felt great to have my apartment, but I did not need it from the bullshit I was doing. I was wildin!!! My friends were smoking and doing other things. I was not as bad as I could have been. I wasn't having sex with anyone at the time. I did not want to just fuck anyone. It was time for me to focus on me and Donny.

I know you guys are wondering what happened to me doing nails. Well, let's go back for a minute. My teacher Mrs. Caldwell decided to open a nail shop. As I stated before, she hired the entire graduating class. One of the students, Candra, and Mrs. Caldwell became partners. Candra was a small frail woman who had Multiple Sclerosis. She was ill. She was weak, skinny, and rarely had an appetite. We all knew something was wrong with her just by looking at her. Candra was married and one would think that was good for her right? Well...stay with me to find out.

Candra's husband Milton was an entertainer, a musician, and a deacon of the church. Sounds good right? Seemed like an honest man who would honor his wife and God. Boy boy boy...looks can be very very deceiving. I do not judge churchgoers, but there is some crooked ass church folk out here. Isn't it funny how they normally are the well-known ones and are full of shit? He didn't fool me. I felt something was strange with him from the start. I just couldn't pinpoint what. Unfortunately, I was about to find out. Candra's husband, Milton, started to flirt with me. I never thought too much into it. I just thought he was just a flirty old man. Note that I was visibly young. I was only 19. He looked to be in his mid-30s at the time. Men flirt all the time. So, it wasn't a big deal to me. I hoped it wasn't serious because I did not know how to handle this. Mom never taught me how to handle any kind of situation like this.

I just avoided him every chance I could. Mainly because I had an issue with saying no to people. I have had this problem since I was a kid and I still have this same problem today. Especially saying no to men. I thought I was supposed to say yes to men. I thought they protect you and give you everything that you need. Boy was I so fucking wrong about this man thing, and besides I was not attracted to him at all. Somehow, he still found me and flirted no matter what I said. I clearly showed him how uninterested I was. I said to him "you're joking right?" and he would say "of course".

One day Candra invited me to come over to their house and have dinner. She was persistent. I made excuse after excuse. At first, I told her no because I was going to my mom's house, or I had to get my son. She asked if I would call my mom for her. She asked my mom if it was okay if she watched Donny for me to come to have dinner. Because they were churchgoers Mom told her, "Yes I have Donny Fee, have nothing to worry about." They only met once or twice at the nail shop. So, I agreed to go over and hang out. I had made up my mind that I was not staying over. I thought to myself, *well I will be fine with all these folk in the house. I know he will not try anything.*

They had a five-year-old son who was so adorable. He was infatuated with me, and he thought I was his girlfriend. They also had a daughter who was about eight years old. The family seemed to have money. Oh my, the house was BIG and beautiful. They had nice cars. They had a piano in the living room. *Oh shit, how cool was that*? I knew right then and there that I wanted to be like them. I wanted them to teach me. I wanted a family and to live a luxurious lifestyle like this.

I was so intrigued by what I saw. I thought I could learn something from them. I was big on learning from the older team. Most older people brought wisdom into conversations. Well, at least that's what the fuck I thought. I thought I would learn something great from them. Oh boy, was I fooled. Get ready because you are in for a treat with this one. I found out how sick these folks were. I do not want to be anything like these crazy mother fuckers. They were beyond perverted. Looks can be very deceiving. I was young and still dumb as hell. I was naïve and knew nothing. I went to their house thinking it was just for dinner and that they would bring me home afterward. Like what I saw on TV shows. Well, that's not what happened. I ended up staying overnight because the wife insisted that I did. They walked me to a room next to little Milton's room.

After dinner, we chatted, talked, entertained playing the piano, and did family shit. I mean they were playing instruments and singing. I had a nice time. I felt safe here. I wish this is how the story ends. It was not. It was now time for bed. I walked to the guest room. I was asleep until I heard the door opening. It was him...Milton. Yes, the creepy, old, flirty, and MARRIED man from the nail salon. He tried to have sex with me.

Oh my God! I am freaking out. My mind was rambling with thoughts all over the place. How could I be so clueless? I didn't see the signs...I could have ran and called my mother to come to get me...I'm still being used. I don't want to be grown anymore... I wish I was taught more... I never listened to all the shit I was being told while I was young. Why didn't I listen? I was being hot in the ass. I thought I knew everything. I KNOW NOTHING!! I didn't know what I was getting myself into this time. This is bad!

It was around 2 am when he woke me up. I jumped out of bed so fast because he scared me. I thought something was wrong. He pulled me down to the floor because his son was in the bed. He kept trying to eat my pussy through my shorts on the floor. I kept saying, NO, *NO your wife is in the other room, and I don't feel comfortable doing this.* He said, "oh it's ok she won't know because she took her meds, and she will not be moving at all any time soon." I replied saying, *well that's my friend and I don't want to do this.* His voice got louder, and he said, "You have to do this!" I screamed *NO!!!!* a thousand times and he kept trying to penetrate me. I said *NO!!* He put his hand over my mouth and said, "it's ok she's fine with it, I do it all the time we have an agreement." I still said *no I am not here for that, and I just want to go home. I* kept saying *I want to go home.*

He did not listen to me and after a while, he ate my pussy, and it was weird as fuck. We had sex it took about five pumps, and it was over. He kept his hand over my mouth the entire time. I was scared as fuck, and I was in complete shock. I didn't know if it was rape or not, but I was just glad it was over. The weirdest part was he left the room and went to his room and had sex with his wife. OMG!!!!!!!!!!! I couldn't believe what was happening. If you could have seen my face. I had tears rolling down my face in shock and fear at the same time. I wanted to go home. I was too scared to go back to sleep.

He acted as if nothing happened the next morning. I did not tell my mom or his wife. I told no one. Who would believe me anyway? Everyone woke up to breakfast, smiles, and good morning attitudes. *It did not happen*, was what I told myself. At this point, I did not want to deal with them at all anymore. I quit the nail shop. Every weekend she called and tried to get me to come to their house. I told her HELL NO!!!!!. They called and called to try and get me to come back to the Nail shop. NOT GOING TO HAPPEN.... I think this was what they did to have a sex life because she was ill. The shit was weird and crazy, I wanted no parts in this at all.

Looking back, 20 years later I remember Candra talked about how she wanted to spice things up in their bedroom. In class, she often talked about wearing lingerie and doing kinky stuff to seduce her husband into having sex. But I didn't think that I was going to be the toy, the foreplay, or whatever the fuck you call it. I guess according to them I was there to spice things up. WRONG! Milton raped me and I am beginning to wonder if Candra knew.

I stayed away from the nail shop for weeks. Guess what? Milton became my stalker. He stalked me for weeks. I had to come up with something to get rid of him. Three weeks later he showed up at my apartment. Man, I forgot...they had dropped me off for work once before. I had no idea he remembered where I lived. Milton asked me if he could talk to me about the nail shop. I talked myself into letting him come in this one time. I let him in because he claimed he wanted to talk about business. *How can I be so naive?* I was older and wiser now. Yeah, so I thought. He sat down on the couch and asked for water. I walked to the kitchen to get him water and when I returned my mouth dropped. I should have known he was full of shit. He had his whole dick out.

I said to him *look I do not want to do this. I do not like you like that. I am going to tell Candra.* He said to me "she doesn't care as long as I am happy." I asked him to *leave,* but he grabbed my hand and pulled me to the couch. We sat there for a minute, and he tried to kiss me. I turned my head. He stood over me and continued to try and kiss me. I kept turning my head and he became unhappy. I said to him loudly *I DO NOT WANT TO HAVE SEX WITH YOU!* " He said, "you know I can't get enough of you; I love you" He then pushed me onto the couch and kept kissing and touching me.

Fear won and I just gave up. I let him get his 4 pumps in and bust a nut. He did not attack me or anything, but I said no at least five times. We fucked as he held my hand down; it turned him on. Afterward, he said nothing and got up and left. No, I did not like it but, I did it. I knew what I was doing. I said NO!! so many times, but somehow, I felt like I consented every time. I didn't enjoy any-thing about him or his looks. I was not sexually attracted to him. He was a dark slender man with a smooth sharp box haircut, but it was something about him that I hated. I even hated how he smelled. *Ugh, He smelled like an OLD MAN.*

As I grew older, I blamed myself for allowing this shit to happen. I do take responsibility for my part in this because I was grown. I could have screamed or told someone. I was just not brave enough to speak. I was weak. I could not say no and stick to it. Once again here I was keeping someone's dirty little secret. I had to figure out a way to get rid of him though. I decided to take my friend's Tee advice and I told him I was pregnant. That was the advice she gave me to get rid of men. He asked me to get an abortion and he gave me the money to have one. I made sure someone was home with me when he brought the money. *I was not ever having sex with his nasty ass again and I WAS NOT PREGNANT*!!! Guess what, I did not see his ass anymore. *Tee's advice worked.* I was so glad because I was tired of being harassed.

I needed a job. One day Mom and I were walking through the jewelry store and this chubby white guy (who looked kind of like John Travolta) came running toward me. He asked if I wanted a job. I was not sure why he chose me, but Mom said, "YES, she would love a job." Well, long story short I got the job and was working in a week. I worked at the jewelry store for a little while until I got in some shit listening to Lee Lee. I seem to always attract drama in the workplace.

Lee Lee was just as small as me. She had a nice shape and was shorter than me. She was a little shy, smiled all the time, energetic, bubbly, and loved to party. She was so nice and friendly to me. I believed she had my best interest at heart. We started hanging out and getting to know one another. I did not think she would steer me wrong. I was wrong. Well, my new friend showed me how to take jewelry without getting caught. She taught me how to *STEAL and Yes, I wanted to do it!* I had never had much and was broke. I wanted to have something. I would not do it for shit at first. I told Lee Lee what I liked, and she stole it for me. I mostly bought my jewelry using my employee discount. There was no excuse for me to take from there because I was getting a great discount. Hell, why spend my money on it when I can do what she was doing?

I was cool with that at first. I was not greedy with it because I was scared to shits. I saw her with her arms loaded with jewelry. I was fascinated by how good it looked on her. So let me tell you what happened to me. I was closing this night. Lee Lee, Kev, and I were there. I told Lee Lee what I wanted, and she did her normal stealing routine. I joined the party this time.

I stole a tennis bracelet, a ring, and a watch. I was so fucking scared to do it. I was so relieved I didn't get caught. After that night I did not steal again. One month later a store audit was done. I did not understand until they called me to come to the police station. The police officer asked me if I took anything. I told him, nope, *no, nope, and no.* My heart was about to burst out of my chest. He told me that Lee Lee told him that she had gotten something. In my head, *I was like how the hell she cracked so quickly?*

So, I told the police officer that I was given some jewelry and I gave them everything I had. I never told them that I took anything. He said that she gave him the same story and that I was innocent. I assumed they didn't know who got what. We later found out that some white girls who worked there had taken so much shit. They blamed it on us. Oh, and they stole some expensive jewelry, and therefore the audit was kicked into high gear. I mean we had taken little petty shit; these bitches were taking the big shit. Thank God we were not charged. We were released the same day. We did not get charged and they let us go. Of course, they didn't want the young white girls to get in trouble or go to jail either. I did not care what happened to them, I was happy we were let off the hook. I did not need a bad record. I was too young.

I learned my lesson and I never stole anything else again. I will not take shit that is not mine. NOTHING. I did not want to go to jail. I was so scared as soon as I saw the police. I just knew I was going to jail. I had been there before for fighting and shit, but I knew this charge would be different.

I did not want to get any serious time for this. I am not about that life. Stealing is not my strong trait and of course, we are *FIRED*. New career me, please!

I was trying to get this shit right and get my life together. At this point, a car was my number one focus. I was willing to do anything. Anything except selling pussy to get me a car. My aunt Glen said if I could get $1500, I could have her 1998 Toyota Camry. I had been driving this car since I was 12. I know…I know… I was too young to drive, but I did anyway. I am a country girl and my family believed in teaching us survival skills young. I was broke as a joke right now and needed to figure out a way to get money. Sid, my friend, was the only friend I had at the time.

I thought Sid was being real with me, but I heard some disturbing rumors. I heard that he told people that we were fucking, had fucked, or I wanted him. We were good friends and honestly, I thought he liked my friend Shon. I knew he messed around with my cousin. So, these rumors were hard for me to believe. I ignored them and I continued to be friends with him. Oh, and for the record; I never fucked him. I saw him as my best friend. He cut my baby Donny's hair for me all the time and we hung out occasionally.

One day, while I was at the barbershop Sid, introduced me to some young ladies there. We all agreed to meet at my house later that night to have drinks and eat. Let me introduce you to these ladies as we will be spending some time together. Kala (also known as Lil Kee-was extremely skinny, short, always wore blonde hair, and her teeth were messed up.) Penny (also known as deep throat. Penny was 5ft 11in tall. She was a big girl, thick, not fine at all, and had a mini afro.) Lisa (also known as Pebbles was thick, cute, with chocolate skin, and she was about my height. Crystal (was short and high yellow to the point where she looked like a white girl. She was small and quiet. She was nice and just wanted to fit in. But for some reason it just seems she talked slowly, and people took advantage of that and picked on her.)

We were all kicking it and having a good time and Lil Kee received a call. I saw the ladies huddled together as they started talking. I overheard Lil Kee talk about making some "quick" money. We all loaded up in the Lil Kee's Ford Explorer truck and went to a spot or should I say an apartment. It was not a club. They changed from regular clothes into stripper outfits. I was looking around confused as hell. I was thinking to myself, *what the fuck is going on*? I thought we were partying, but I was feeling it. I just went with the flow. Well, Lil Kee and Penny were having a good time dancing, smoking, yelling, grinding, popping bottles, and making some major money. That's what they thought. Niggas were smiling, touching, smoking, and throwing money. I just wanted the money. My brain went into overload and little flags went up *like they were not selling pussy, but they were making money...hmmmmmmm When* we returned to my apartment and all the partying was over, I was eager to ask questions. I had plenty of them. *Do you guys make a lot of money every time you guys go out to dance? How often do you guys do this? Do you guys have sex for money doing this or do they expect sex?*

These ladies answered my questions, but never stopped counting their money. Money is exactly what I was looking for. I needed some freaking money for a car. I was tired of walking with my baby in the stroller to the doctor and the grocery store for milk. I was tired of walking everywhere, period. Oh, and they finally popped the question. *Do you want to do it next time?* I was like, *HELL YEA*! I was down. I needed this car. I was desperate!! To be honest I was scared as hell and did not know anything about dancing. I knew when I drank enough, I would be ok with shaking a little ass. The guys there asked who I was and why was I not dancing. Lil Kee and Sid asked me the same question "why not make this money?" They are asking to see you, Fee. I wanted to make some cash to get this car already. So, yes, I did want to go and get loose. I wanted to make some of this money they kept talking about. So, call me Anxious, the stripper.

I went shopping for outfits, boots, lingerie, thongs, or anything to help me look good for my big night. I wanted to be ready. I was terrified, scared, and ashamed. I looked good and I knew I could do this!! The only thing I kept thinking about was me WALKING!! I was tired of being broke. I was tired of not having shit at all. Yes, I graduated from high school and nail school. But I still needed more. I was proud of my accomplishments, but I needed more money. I needed more money quickly.

I became a stripper. I stripped for private shows. It was mostly house calls for a group of men looking for a good time and wanting to see some ass. My first gig was at a house with a bunch of thirsty ass men hanging all around. I was so freaking nervous. I did not know what to do with myself. I knew how to dance, I was flexible, I had the body, and I was cute. I was just freaking scared. I wore a pair of black thongs and a bra Penny let me borrow. It had shingles on it. I wore all black with boots that came to my knees. We danced and made money. I made about $250 my first night and I was happy with that.

For the next gig, we went to this big-ass barn/man cave type of shit. It was a real barn in the country. It was a nice man cave. It had a bar, bathroom, seats, drinks, music, and dance floor. It looked like a nice club. I made hella money that night! It was so much that all of it could not fit in my boot. I never let anyone hold on to my money. I saw men all over me. They threw money all over me. I felt like somebody! I was 20 years old and hungry. I hung from the ceiling and oh I was much more flexible than I thought. I was that bitch. I was hungry for money, power, and success!!!

I looked over and saw Noot, a friend of my old boyfriend KT. I trusted Noot and he was a familiar face. I let him hold some of my money. I learned that he was a snake. Snakes change and camouflage all the time. At the end of the night, he gave me $200, and I knew I gave him way more than that. I was so glad I kept most of my money stuffed in my boots. Hell, I'm glad I even wore knee boots because they came in handy. That nigga had nothing else to say to me. Why would you steal a little chump change from a girl? That is a definition of a pussy ass nigga. He was a pussy ass nigga. I later found out that he was the mole to set every nigga up on the block including KT because he was a jealous nigga.

Oh, and it gets worse! I later found out that most of the other girls were making a lot more money than me. *Guess how... Yes!* They fucked and sucked on the low. They were selling pussy the entire time. The guys that were there knew what they were coming for. It seemed as if that's what they were known for. Especially Penny. She seemed to be Ms. Professional of the operation. I guess that's where she got the name deep throat from. These ladies smoked weed and other things. I did not want any parts in that. Smoking weed was not my thing. I know you heard of the popular saying "birds of a feather flock together" well not me! I did not want to be part of that flock of birds. I was NOT selling my ass. I am not that type of girl. I had to stop fucking with them quickly especially when I found out they were doing coke on top of that. These ladies said Sid was sniffing powder also. I couldn't believe it. I knew he was a smoker but damn. I thought he was trying to do better for himself. Coke was not the way. Well anyway, I made about $600 that night and I was DONE!!!!

I was still on a mission to get myself a car and that's all I thought about. My aunt gave me the car anyway and I gave her $1000 and $200 a month. I was happy and did not need to do any extra dancing. I did try out a strip club. It was called Sammie's Showgirls strip club. I danced for a hot three weeks. I saw my friend Shon there and I could not believe it. We were inseparable at one point. Hell, that's how I met Donny's daddy. We reconnected for a short time. I later heard she moved to Georgia. A few weeks later Sid introduced me to another girl named Candy. She was a small petite girl about 5ft 3in tall. She looked much taller with heels on. She always had them on. She was a very pretty girl, but she seemed a little weird if you ask me. She acted as if she was on something. Who am I to judge? She was a hustler who knew how to get her money dancing or selling whatever she needed to sell.

I began to think deeper into my life. I wanted someone who could offer me something, help me get on the right path, be stable enough to make me a wife, and live a good life. I noticed that it seemed as if I looked for a dad in every nigga I met. I wonder if it's because I lacked a father in my life. I have never had true fatherly love before. Especially from my real blood father. Let's be clear I DO NOT blame him for the decisions and choices I made in my life. I blame myself for all of that. I've always dated older men. I knew exactly what to expect from them; that's what I thought. It seems that my dreams were just that. Older men seemed to treat me better than younger guys. I felt that younger guys were immature. Most of them seemed to be into looks and wanted pretty girls. I felt that most guys never saw me as wifey material. They seem to only want one thing: the cat. *Yes, it's true.*

I did not think I was pretty. I was insecure, did not like myself, and thought I was ugly. I was bullied in school, and it still haunts me to this day. I was told that I was ugly a lot. I had low self-esteem. I was used by men, or should I say I let men use me. I blamed myself for anything that happened to me. *Why did I blame myself?* I was beating myself up over my flaws. I thought I had a lot of flaws. Most of them were made up in my head. I'm sure if I had felt special during my childhood, I would feel better about myself.

Oh, I forgot to mention that a few weeks earlier Sid introduced me to this cool older cat named Mel. Mel was a sharp and cool dude. He had a nice ride. You know everyone was looking at niggas rides back then. He had a nice dark green Nissan Maxima with rims. He had been in the military and had been a mortician. He dressed nice, had a good job, smelled good, looked good and he was nice. I was interested in what he had to offer then in my life. Mel was very interesting. I also thought he was strange. The type of strange that made me curious enough to get to know him better. I liked him even though I thought he was conceited. He thought he was the shit. Mel knew he was somebody in this world and no one could tell him otherwise. He had a lot going on for himself. He played instruments, was mature, and he spoke his mind.

Sid was a regular at my house by this time. He stopped by every day after work. The barber shop was right across the street. One day he came in while I was laying on the couch watching television. I did not know he had someone with him. Then walks in Mel with his serious face on. I did not pay him any mind because I thought he was one of Sid's friends. I got off the couch to check on the roast beef I was cooking. Mel said "it smells good in here. "I said, *thank you*. Sid said to Mel "you ready." He looked like yes but no.

The next day Sid told me that Mel said he had to have me. He did not ask me on a date, but we spent a lot of time with one another after that. I mean every day he was at my house. I guess you can say our first date was me cooking the same roast beef with gravy over rice for him. He took me around an older crowd, and it was different. It was different to be around people that had good things going on in their life. One of his friends worked with the funeral home with his family. His other friends were veterans and business owners. After about three weeks we were hot and heavy on one another. It started with just kissing and you know what they say, you can tell when the sex is going to be good from a kiss. Or should I say you can tell when a nigga can eat some pussy by the way they kiss.

Mom kept Donny a lot. I had to fuss with her to even get him sometimes. She was so in love with her first grandchild. She always wanted him there with her. I did not argue with her. Sometimes Donny would ask to go with her. I had Donny all week and my mom came to get him for the weekend. Great because Mel is coming over and I did not want them to meet yet. After Mel finished eating, he was so excited about the food I cooked. He said it was so good and he never had anything like it. He went on and on about how great I was and wondered why I was not taken already. I told him I'm too young for all that and men don't want a good woman. He looked me in my eyes and said, "well I do." It was over from there.

We were sitting on the couch at this time. We started kissing, and it was hot and heavy. He licked and sucked on my neck. This took me somewhere because THAT WAS MY SPOT!!! Ohhhhhhh YES!! I was completely turned on at this point and there was no stopping. Mel was all over me and I loved it. I mean my body was feeling things that I never felt before. It seemed that he wanted me to feel great and he was on a mission of just that. He started peeling my clothes off piece by piece and I did not stop him. I helped him.

I told him to let's go upstairs to the bedroom. Now I lay there naked on the bed, and he looked at me as if I was a little snack. He came closer to me, and I could feel his breath and his beard on my neck. I could feel all the juices forming between my legs. His lips were at my right nipple then my left. Ohhhh the feelings I was having were amazing. I could feel him going further down past my belly button. All the juices that were forming he liked. He watered his beard with it. Wow, I felt a tingling feeling that I had never had before, and it felt great. He lifted my legs and licked every part of my pussy that I didn't even know I had. I didn't get a chance to return the favor. Now you know I love to suck a good clean dick. Within seconds he had a condom on, and he was diving into my walls. He was stroking and moving like a dancer. He turned me over and went crazy. This dick was so good. We were sweaty and sticky when it was all over, but well worth it. OH MY!!! The sex was great with Mel. He was nasty!!!

We were stuck like glue after that. I tried almost everything sexually with him EVERYTHING!! I was comfortable with him. I let him fit his dick in every hole I had except my ear. He loved some feet! Yes, he did. He sucked my toes. It was not my thing, but I was aiming to please. So, I let him suck and rub anytime he wanted to. Mel sucked my toes and his dick got rock hard.

I began to trust him that much to explore. I fell for him hard, and he fell for me. I knew he was falling for me. He was too hard-core to show his feelings or tell me how he felt about me. You know how niggas want to just show that they are hard, and they are the shit no matter what. That was Mel. He said to me often "as long as you come home nothing else matters." Oh, but when we were in the bedroom, he showed me all kinds of love from the top of my head to the bottom of my feet. Now don't get me wrong, I knew he loved me. He just showed me differently. He made the mistake of not showing me love. He took me for granted. He never showed me love in front of people. Because I was young, he thought he could say and do what he wanted. He thought he could talk and flirt with other girls.

His ex-girlfriend Tina was a problem and he felt it was okay for him to deal with her whenever he wanted to. You know how it is; men don't want to break the code and look like they love a woman. Most men want to be hard and look like they control the relation-ship. He had it like that for a few minutes. They try to impress their boys. It's funny because most of these men are doing the same thing. Showing their soft side to their women, but hard in front of their friends. Mel was very strong-minded, and he felt the need to show that he didn't care for me. If you met him, you would know exactly what I mean. Overall, I knew he was a good dude inside and out.

I was comfortable with Mel, and we had been dating for a few months. The dancer Candy had a gig at the hotel and literally begged me to go with her. She did not want to go alone, and they wanted two girls at the hotel that night. I said to her, No! *I'm done with dancing. Shit, I'm chilling 'tonight. I want to smooch with my Mel.* Mel looked at me and said, "I will go with you baby just get your money and I'll be your security guard. You're too sexy to turn it down." *Okay!!!* He kinda turned me on. So, we went to this hotel and had some drinks.

We chilled because there was not much money to be made. There weren't many people there. I was bored and the niggas in there were bored too. Then a proposition came across the table from one of the guys for us to make $500. He said he wanted to see something he had never seen before. I looked around like I had no clue what they wanted to happen. They knew I wasn't selling any ass. I am not a prostitute. Back in the 2000s $500 was a lot of money. Of course, you know I had to ask a few questions. I needed the money, so I was curious.

So here was the deal…*The deal or the fetish was that they wanted to see Candy eat me out.* I was quick to say NO!!! I said no because I immediately had a flashback of my childhood. I was molested by a girl and was not feeling that shit.

I was not into being with a female and it had never crossed my mind. I mean at all. Even if I did it, I probably will have flashbacks of my childhood trauma. Mel convinced me to do it. He was such a smooth talker, and he knew how to get to me. He promised to hold my hand the entire time. Trust me, it was like pulling teeth. Because I did not want to do it. Mel was on one end trying to convince me and Candy was on the other end begging. Sid was on the far end saying come on Fee. The young girl in me was thinking about the money. *Okay Okay, I gave in.* I decided to let her eat me out so I could get paid. I drove 45 minutes there to get paid. I was embarrassed and I hoped that I would not regret this.

I laid down on the bed and she slipped my thong off. She started licking and sucking on me like it was not her first time. NOT HER FIRST TIME!!! She did it with no problem. It didn't do much for me. It was nice and it felt good. Not bad at all, but not my cup of tea. I probably would do it again for the right price and with the right person. But let's just say the guys in the room were turned on and up!!! ESPECIALLY my nigga. He was so turned on and smiled all night. We were quiet on the whole ride home. He just looked and smiled at me almost the whole time. But, as soon as we walked into the house and showered, he completely attacked me. When I said attacked me, it was an attack that I liked and enjoyed.

It was like a whole porn movie, and he was the star. I let him do whatever he wanted. I was kind of tipsy as well. It was well worth it cause I was shaking all night. Mel always took care of my body, mind, and holes. He took total control over my body. He took his time with me and my body. He was so nasty and knowledgeable, and I loved it. I let him do whatever he wanted to cause the shit was completely a turn-on. It felt like I got my adult wings. We were great together and I was in love with him. I treated him like he was my man, my king, my everything.

I learned how much I liked sucking dick when I was with Mel. I liked sucking dick. It did something to me and my soul. Oh, the taste, the meat, the suck, slobbering, my lips around it, the moans while my mouth is full. Sucking dick was something I love doing and I knew I was great at it. Yes, I said it, I suck dick and I know I suck dick well. If I didn't know anything else, I knew I could suck a good old dick real good. Mel knew as well. It all just turned me on to satisfy him. For me, I liked the feeling of being in control at that moment. If I knew I was satisfying you; then I knew I was in control. I took advantage of it. It is so funny how back in the day guys and girls lied about eating pussy or sucking dick. NOT ME!!! I love it.

Mel and our relationship were too good to be true. Of course, there had to be drama somewhere in the equation. So let me tell you the story. My ex-drug dealer boyfriend KT sent me some jail mail. Guess who it was about? Mel. He had the urge to tell me about Mel. I felt that he was jealous and did not want me to be happy. That is usually how it went with exes. But deep down inside I knew he was protective of me and did not want anyone to play me. I knew it was coming sooner or later because he still wanted me. He thought I was still his and he wanted to control me.

KT knew almost everyone in Kinston, so the news usually got back to him. So, whatever KT knew he was going to tell me. He told me that Mel was cheating on me with his ex-girlfriend. I'm sure you want to know how he knew. Here is how. The girl who combed twisted Mel's hair knew KT. She told him and he told me. Mel kept his hair maintained more than I did so I felt it could be true. KT gave me the girl's address and everything. I did not believe him at first. I kept it from Mel. A week or so had passed by and Mel started acting a little funny. He disappeared and did not answer his phone for hours. I said to myself *if he disappears again, I am going to this address that KT gave me.*

A few days later I called and called and called several times repeatedly and he would not answer. You already know what I did after that. I went on a little field trip to the address. He had no clue that I knew. Lord beholds look whose green Nissan Maxima I saw. His car was very distinctive, so I knew it was him. I called, but still no answer. So, I called about 10-20 times back-to-back. It would go to voicemail or maybe he just wouldn't answer. I called over and over with no answer. I sat outside watching and waiting for him to come out. I was mad and yelling in my head, I KNOW YOU SEE ME CALLING YOU! If it was nothing going on, why couldn't he just answer my calls? I went home pissed. He was too good to be true. I knew something was bound to happen. Okay, now like I said before, I was a very revengeful person. I would not let a man control me, make me look stupid, or screw whoever they wanted.

After this episode, I talked to him and expressed to him my thoughts and concerns. He told me his ex would always be in his life because her child is like his child. He said that he was over there spending time with her child. He also said he will always love her because she is like his best friend. Ohhhhh shit, that shit flowed out his mouth like he did not care a fuck. Oh, you must think you got a dummy. I was not stupid at all. I knew he was going to come up with something, but this was not a good answer at all. That was not a good excuse for me because it made me look bad.

My man was coming up with all kinds of lies for her. Well...he didn't know I knew the game already. I was young but I DAMN sure was not all the way dumb. One of his famous lines was "in life, you have to deal with shit or let it go." I said to myself I can do three things; Either I can leave it, love it, or stay above it. I chose to stay. I stayed and kept dealing with him and his bullshit. But it was short-lived. I told myself that I was not going to keep dealing with this shit. I'm too young. Oh...*It's on now because I've been nice long enough.*

One day, Tee and I were at the club chilling and having a good time and a guy named Brian walked in flirting. He rubbed against me, and I felt this big hard something on my back. He was much taller than me and tall is good to me. I can look up at a nigga. OH MY GOD, IT WAS SO BIG AND I CAN TELL!! Not unbearably big but big. I could handle that shit. *I tell you what though if it's over 10 inches I am running.* I like my insides and do not want my coochie stretched like the Mississippi river. I was laughing at myself and shit. I wanted to fuck him so bad, but you know me. I still was trying to be a good girl for my man. Even though he ain't shit right now. Oh, and by the way, I hadn't seen Mel in a few days. He was in and out claiming he had to go take care of some family stuff. We talked a little here and there. They were dry chats on the phone. Mel has not learned that ex's only come back around when they see you happy with the next one. I'm sure he will learn his lesson a little too late.

For weeks I avoided Brian because I knew I was weak and vulner-able. I couldn't avoid him anymore. I needed some attention and Mel wasn't around as much anymore. He was not the Mel I fell in love with and right now Brian is here. He was around and gave me the attention I'd been craving for weeks from my man. Mel was sup-posedly going out of town for this weekend. He and his homeboys were going to DC. I was not pressed at all. I am a homebody, and I knew what was meant for me will be mine. What is NOT meant for me God will take it away from my eyes. I was okay. I loved sitting home, watching television, sitting on the porch, listening to the rain, and cooking. Whatever Mel had going on was on him because I was not the dummy, he thought he had. I had no problem with him doing whatever he wanted to do. However, I guarantee you will not disrespect me or have me looking stupid.

I did not tell Brian that Mel was going out of town. Somebody else did or maybe he knew that Mel had not been around. So, let me say this; when you have a nice woman and other men see that, they are watching and preying. They are waiting for the opportunity to shoot their shot. I'm sure Tee told Brian that I was home alone. She was the only big-headed ass I told. I was enjoying my alone time. I put my Razac lotion on and cooked myself a small meal. I cooked two pieces of fried chicken, mac & cheese, and some green beans. I was laid back, chilling and watching TV. I thought I was about to do my usual alone time routine. I thought I was ready to write in my notebook and then fall asleep. I was interrupted by a knock on the door. *Who could this be?* I wasn't expecting anyone. I thought it was Sid passing through from the barbershop to see if I had leftovers or some. I most definitely was going to send his ass home. I opened the door, rolling my eyes and it was BRIAN!!! Yes, Brian...my weakness. Oh, how I needed it not to be him!

I was in shock and didn't know what to do or say. I was thinking to myself, what *do you want nigga*? He walked in without an invitation or without saying a word. *Oh my!* He smelled so good and looked hella good too. Tall, 6 ft 4 in *you know I love a tall man*, sexy, caramel, and nice body. *Oh shit.* I was sweating and nervous. My hands were cold. I asked him in a serious tone, what *do you want and how did you know I was home*? I tried to be hardcore and stand my ground, but my heart was about to beat out of my chest. I knew what was about to happen. I was acting like I never had dick before or should I say that size dick before. I will never forget that beautiful sight.

I was facing the door and I closed the door behind him. I waited for a second and took a few deep breaths. As I turned around to say *why are you here?* He was right there at my nose and it kind of scared me. I started to back up. He grabbed me close to him and started tonguing me down. *Oh my, what is happening???* He grabbed the back of my neck gently, but sternly. He grabbed me as he wanted me right then and there. His hands were so strong and large. I was half his size, so he was kind of roughing me up and I was turned all the way on. At first, I pushed away and said *NO I can't.* I knew damn well I wanted that shit bad as fuck. I dropped my head and said *I can't. I'm still involved with someone.* He said, "where is he because he's not here." He had a point. I thought to myself, where *is Mel*?

Brian grabbed me and started kissing me in a way that I had never experienced before. He started licking and sucking my neck. I was so turned on. Then he dropped to his knees and started eating my pussy like it was food. Noodles to be exact!!!! Because he was slurping and licking. I was shivering and dripping wet. I could feel it fall down my leg. I could not continue standing any longer. He picked me up and laid me on the couch. Brian continued to devour my pussy. He moved his way up and started sucking on my titties and then kissed me again. I loved how he kissed me, and the taste of my pussy was so good to me. All I could do was moan because it was feeling so fucking good. His dick was so hard in his pants I had to pull it out and suck it. It was my thing, I loved sucking dick! It was so fucking pretty. I sucked it with passion, hunger, and control. I was reminded at this moment of why I loved sucking dick. I loved hearing the moans and the enjoyment. He gave me all of that. I loved to hear him moan. I pushed him onto the couch and asked if he had a condom because getting pregnant was not on my mind at all. I was ready. I was so ready to feel him inside of me.

He put on a condom, and I stood on my tippy toes. I sat right in his lap slowly and I let his large meat fit into my tight hole. After letting the tip go in a few times it was completely ready. His dick was drenched with my wetness. The more he moaned and grabbed me the wetter I became. I was dripping wet. It slid in and out of my young tight pussy. He could not stop looking at me. I grabbed the back of his head and rode for dear life. We both were moaning and shaking like a leaf because it was so freaking good. He laid his head on my breast and I held my head back because I was enjoying every throbbing sensation going through my pussy. He had his hands on my hips and was holding on for the ride. It didn't take him long to explode as I was biting his lip and staring him in his eyes. I could feel his dick throbbing inside me. I knew it was over and his body collapsed. I looked up at him and I softly said to him *we can't do this anymore.* (IIis dick was still inside of me) I laid on his chest for a few. He said "fuck that I am getting some more of that. It was worth waiting for" He then said to me "please tell me I can have some more." I said *maybe*, but I knew I was going to run from him.

I could not let this happen again. Yes, it was so GREAT! I enjoyed every lick, every stroke, every ache, every kiss, every nut, and every position. EVERYTHING was awesome and I honestly do not know how I feel about it. BUT I do know I cannot do this again. Mel would be crushed if he knew I had fucked somebody else. Yes, even though he was fucking with someone else. I still cared about him. I still loved him.

Three days later Mel came back around and started acting like he had some sense. *Was it too late?* Because it still didn't seem the same. A piece of me was gone. I kind of felt when Mel changed. I noticed that pieces of him were missing. He had been fucking someone else and they probably shifted his ass to the side. I felt so bad about what I did, but on the other hand, I didn't feel bad at all. I would not have cheated if he had not done it first. All I wanted from him is to put me first and not do whatever he was doing with his ex. Truthfully, I didn't know what he had going on or why he insisted on staying with me. BUT I knew he was dealing with someone else and wanted us both! He did not want to have to choose.

Mel ran his mouth while getting his hair braided every other week. His so-called homie spilled the tea to KT and said that Mel was bragging about cheating as if it was cool. I hope it was worth it. So, I was curious to know why suddenly, he wanted to be here. I guess his ex-girlfriend found a new boyfriend or something because he started acting like he wanted to be with me. Deep down I was sure he knew not to fuck with me... I mean did he think I would not get his ass back. Funny and the joke was on him! Because he had me FUCKED UP!!

CHAPTER 5

Do Not Drink and Drive

Mel and I were not on good terms. Our relationship was close to death. So, when my aunt Trina came to visit for a few days from Henderson, it was exactly what I needed. She was going through a few things and needed a getaway. I needed a getaway and we decided to hang out. My apartment was the getaway for anyone from my hometown. We both needed to get out of the house for a few. Trina and I went to this club called Jay's to see some male strippers. They never came to this small ass town, so we had to go. It was a must. We were drinking and having a good time like we normally did whenever we linked up. I was the drinker, and she was the smoker. I drank too much! I wish I would have let Trina drive because she did not drink much at all.

On the way home I got freaking pulled over and I was 10 seconds from my apartment. A two-minute walk. *What the Fuck!* OMG!! I am scared to shits. I knew I had been drinking a lot. So many thoughts ran through my mind. *I shouldn't have, I'm underage, I am in trouble now.* He steps out of the car and headed toward my car. *YES! the same car that I worked hard for.* He was a short white man with a shiny bald head. The lights on his car reflected on his head. He looked goofy but nice. His uniform seemed to be too big for him. I heard him say "can I see your license and registration, ma'am? It looks like someone had stolen the sticker off your tags." I looked at him scared, cross-eyed, and drunk. I feared the next question, but I knew it was coming. "Have you been drinking?" I was not a good liar. I was sure he smelled the hard brown liquor on my breath. He asked me to step out of the car to do the breathalyzer. Of course, I failed!!! I was headed right to jail.

I was so disappointed in myself. I drove five minutes to get home and get a DUI. The officer was cool as fuck don't get me wrong, but I guess not cool enough to let me walk home. My aunt drove my car back to my apartment. I was so glad she was with me because I avoided my car getting towed. This was my fuck up! I was learning to take responsibility for my wrong choices and faults. I messed up big time and I needed help. Mel was no help. I called him and he was in Washington D.C with his "brothers." Now I was really scared because I only had one other person to call to get me out of jail. I called the pastor. *Oh shit,* and I was scared to call her. Pastor of all Pastors, Mrs. Mommy Martha. I knew I would not hear the end of it. I didn't know what to expect from her. She was like a light switched off and on.

I was happy to see her. She had on a dress suit like the ones she wore to church, her heels of course, and her crooked big ass church hat. Dressed for the occasion. Most importantly, she had her bible in her hand. She bailed me out on bond. The bond was $1000, and she paid $100. She cursed and prayed my ass all the way home. She did not let up and I sat there with my mouth shut. I listened. I could not say a damn word because I was wrong, and I knew I had screwed up. So, the best thing to do was just listen to my mother. Truthfully no matter how right or wrong she had been; she had every right to cuss me out this time. *I must do better,* was what I told myself. I had court a few days later. I needed to prepare for the consequences.

Now it was time for court, and I was shaking in my boots. I did not know what to expect. When I was younger, I went to jail for being in fights. It was for a short period, and I knew this would be a little different. I was an adult now and I could get jail time. Once again Mom came into court with her bible, her church outfit, and her church hat tilted to the side. You gotta love Martha! When I saw her, I immediately had a flashback. She came to my school looking the same way. She was so pissed because I tried to fight someone with canned goods in my bookbag. Nevertheless, I was thankful she was here with me. She prayed as she walked to her seat. She made me more nervous and terrified. I was so embarrassed for putting us in this situation. I was told several times to stop drinking and driving. As you can see, I was hard-headed and did not listen. I looked up and I was scared as hell because it seemed as if she sent everyone to jail, community service, or probation. I did not want any of these punishments. I wanted a fine and just wanted to go back to my tiny apartment.

Oh my! It's my turn. I heard my name "Felicia Hargrove." The judge read my charges and I looked over at Mom. She looked at me in disgust. She had the mean church lady look. I didn't look back at her again. The officer that arrested me spoke highly of me and said I was cooperative with him. He said I was honest about everything. He told the judge that he did not pull me over for reckless driving, swerving, or anything like that. "She was pulled over due to someone taking her sticker off her tags." He told her that I did not give him any trouble at all. He helped me out a lot. The judge asked Ms. Hargrove do you know what you are being charged with?" I said *yes ma'am.*

My mother said, "judge I'm her mother may I speak?" the judge said, "yes" my mother said "before you make your decision on Felicia, she took the ASVAB test for the military and passed. Felicia told me that she did not want to go. She has a date to leave for the Navy." The judge looked at me and said, "oh really Ms. Hargrove, is this true?" I replied saying "yes ma'am." The Judge said "I will give you two options. You can do 60 days in jail or go to the military since you have already taken the test. Your license will be suspended for a year. If you go into the military a year will pass in no time. You will be good and ready to fix everything in a year. So, Ms. Hargrove, what is it going to be?" I said *ma'am I will go to the military because 60 days will not work for me.* The judge looked over at my mom and said "Please let me know if she does not go. Because then she will start her 60 days in jail" My mother said, "I sure will judge" and then I heard the gavel hit the bench.

I went home and had a drink or five because I was so glad that shit was over. I had to leave my son here and I hated it. I knew he would not be raised the way I wanted him to. Well, this was all my fault!!! I had to accept the consequences. It was time for me to make a life change for my son. I hadn't been making good choices for us anyway. I met with my recruiter and told him it was time for me to go. I needed to do better. I then realized how out of shape I was. There was no way I would pass the physical fitness test at Bootcamp. Running was not my strong trait. The next day I ran from my apartment to my mom's house. It was about four miles away. I had two months to get ready. My leave date was May 1, 2001. I was not a runner and I got tired quickly. I was afraid of failing because I had to pass. I had too much on the line. I did not want to go to jail. I had to push myself every single day.

The military could be a good life change for me and Donny. I did not want to leave him, but I knew it was best for us both. Donny was the only reason I was still alive. I owed him a better life, a better understanding of life, and a real family. I would do anything for Donny. I wanted better for him. This is a cruel world, and I will not leave him here to find out for himself. I was focused on leaving and making a better life for us. I gave my mom power of attorney for my baby boy. That was the only way. My son meant the world to me, and no one can change that. I never knew love until I had my Donny.

Well, now it was time to talk to Mel about me leaving for the military. I would be gone for at least four years. I signed up secretly. I felt that it was ultimately my decision. He had been in the military, and I thought he would understand. I didn't know how he would feel. During our conversation, He said "once you leave for the military, we will be over because you will have so many other options. You will catch someone's eye, or someone will catch my eye before it's all over." He often made jokes about me leaving. He said, "have your fun but make sure you come home to me".

Our relationship had been rocky lately and it seemed as if he did not want to be with me. I could tell that he loved me because he was getting a little emotional as the time grew closer for me to leave. *Why did it take for me to leave for him to show me this type of love?* I had been craving this love the whole time. I knew that there was more to life, and I knew it was not here in North Carolina. I could not stay in Kinston forever. I refused to stay here. I will not be a part of my family's generational curse. I planned to break the cycle.

I saw a better life for myself. My entire family was stuck in North Carolina. Most were not doing anything productive or positive. They were being crooked in the church, selling drugs, molesting children, fucking their cousins, being drug addicts, and so on and so on. I wanted more for myself and staying here was not where I was going to get it. I must become somebody and have something in life. I will not sit around here and have babies by no good men. I can't keep short-changing myself. For so long my mind was programmed to stay where I felt comfortable. I know YOU can relate! But there is so much more out in the world to see. We are not taught to go for it and learn new things. The world is not just where we were born. It was time for me to go explore.

CHAPTER 6

Time To Go

The time has come!! May 1, 2001, came very fast and I was on my way to Bootcamp. It was the hardest thing I ever had to do in my life. My Donny stood there looking at me and he was clueless about what was yet to come. He did not know where I was going or when I was coming back. Leaving my son and my apartment was tough. I was hurting inside, and I wished my baby could come with me. I had learned to hold my feelings inside so no one could see my pain. I sucked all my emotions up and reminded myself of this: *I HAD TO DO THIS FOR MY SON. THIS WAS MY ONLY OPTION.*

My recruiter Jackson came to pick me up from Mom's house in a white four-door Ford Taurus. There was another girl named Ciara there. She was a young white girl about 19. And we talked for about 20 minutes during the ride. We introduced ourselves and then were in silence for the remainder of the ride. The ride was an hour and 20 minutes. The first stop was at the Military Entrance Processing Station (MEPS) in Raleigh, North Carolina. I had to get scanned in, take a drug test, and do various other tests. I stayed in one of the cheapest hotels ever. I was terrified and didn't want to go, but I wasn't the type of person to speak up. I usually rolled with whatever most people told me. Meeting new people was interesting and I was glad I did not try to run. Deep down inside I knew this decision was best for me in so many ways. I believe that most of you agree. Yes! Everything came back clear, and it was time for me to transport to my next destination. I was scared. Reality had set in and there was no turning back.

A black clean new looking Chevrolet Tahoe was waiting to take us to the airport. This was my first flight ever and it was to Chicago, Illinois. The plane ride was extremely scary. The plane was shaky, turbulent, and felt like a roller coaster. At this point, I was scared as crap. Oh, and by the way, I HATE roller coasters. Once the flight landed there was a bus waiting for us. Flights were coming from everywhere. I couldn't believe my eyes. There were so many young women and men that had joined the Navy. The bus was extremely full, and I saw people from all over the world. I was nervous. I stayed quiet and waited until I was spoken to. The bus took us to the Bootcamp facility. My fear kicked in at this moment. As soon as we stepped foot off the bus, we heard a whole lot of screaming, yelling, and giving orders.

There was no time wasted. The trainers and officers separated the boys from the girls and told us to follow the booths. Each officer told us what to do. They yelled at us as if we were toddlers. The officers then took all our belongings. EVERYTHING. We were then stripped naked. We were given underwear, a sports bra, socks, a white t-shirt, sweatpants, tennis shoes, and a toiletry bag. The next stop was haircuts for everyone *shoulder length for girls and all off for boys.* I braided my hair thinking that the officers would not cut it, but the female officer cut my hair straight across shoulder length. She didn't care what hair they cut off.

The recruiter told me if I braided my hair that they would not cut it. That was a lie. Of course, it wasn't just me it was everyone that got a haircut. This was the beginning of my discipline and boy did I learn on my first day. My first day was very interesting and informative. I learned how to follow instructions and listen. We were then taken to our bonkers. Then there was non-stop running!!! We ran from Point A to B. We had to run everywhere they told us to go. There was no walking. Pretty scary situation.

We were all assigned to an RDC (Recruit Division Commander) which is the same as a drill Sergeant, we had a lady named Florenzi and she was HELL!! She liked me for some reason, and she encouraged me the entire way. Don't get me wrong, she gave me hell too. Sometimes she said hurtful things to me when she was upset. I guess it was meant to make me stronger, but it hurt. One day, she asked where my father was, and I told her that I did not know him. She then said "I know why he left you. It is because you are weak." OUCH! She told me that I belonged there and that I had potential. I still had to follow rules and get hardcore training just like everyone else. In the military, we were given only two-three minutes to shower and get dressed. If anyone broke the rules everyone received punishment. This was the first step of being a team. We learned the importance of working together and how our individual choices affect the whole team.

If you were brave enough to fuck up, then you should be prepared to sleep with one eye open. Because you could potentially get your ass beat for messing up too many times. We learned to march together, walk together, talk together, sing together, shower together, eat together, get dressed together, and even shit together. It was all about teamwork. There were no questions asked and we did what was told. Our uniforms had to be always squared away. Sweatpants and t-shirts were considered our uniform. We had to earn the nicer uniforms. They were all blue with the United States Navy on the shirts. I was very tired! There were times we stayed up for 24 hours. I knew it was preparing us for battle station. Battle Stations are the capstone event that recruits must pass before graduation. It was to test our knowledge and skills in basic seamanship, damage control, firefighting, and emergency response procedures. In case there was an emergency aboard a naval ship. Sometimes they would wake us up at 3 am to run, march, or work out. Again, it was preparation.

The food was horrible. It was like a sloppy joe kind of thing. However, the shit was good to us because we didn't have anything else to eat. I pretended it tasted like steak and potatoes. We had two-three minutes to eat and whatever we did not finish was thrown away. I was so ready to quit!!! I was used to good food and because of this horrible experience food means everything to me today. A good meal is amazing, and I do not take it for granted. My mother cooked well when she felt like it. I cooked a lot when I was home. I was used to cooking a roast, rice, gravy, and green beans. Cooking was one of my favorite things to do. I was good at it, and we always ate well. I had a hard time adjusting.

I cried a lot during Bootcamp. I was sore from running, marching, yelling, screaming, and working out. One day we were forced to drink all the water out of our canteen. Canteen is a military water bottle. It was a part of our uniform. We were forced to march and drink all our water until we did the routine right. That was the worst day ever. Most of us peed on ourselves because we could not get that shit right. It was cold and snowy. I was so mad and there was nothing I could do about it. We finally got it right and it seemed like it took us forever. This experience taught me more discipline, anger control, strength, and the value of life. I needed this discipline. I was learning differently, and this was beginning to make me different in a good way.

I met a very spunky and outspoken young lady named Blackman from New York at Bootcamp. We were sent everywhere together. We were inseparable. Maybe we were separated for a moment, but even then, we felt love for each other. They somehow would put us back together again. We received a new RDC named Robin. He kind of looked like Cedric the Entertainer. He was short and stocky. He was dark skinned and had moles all over his face. He looked mean as fuck. He ran our ass all day and all night. Blackman and I built a great friendship and where I went, she went, and vice versa. Who she fussed and had beef with I fussed and had beef with? *One band, one sound.* She was the mouthpiece and the firecracker. I was the shy one and the fighter. We fought together, we showered together, we ate together, we cried together, we got in trouble together a lot, and we even learned to swim together. What I didn't have she had and what she didn't have I had. Whatever we did not have, we found together.

I started thinking about Mel and our relationship. I was still hurt, and I still felt the need to get revenge. I knew that two wrongs *don't make it right,* but it did make it even!!! This was my theory and I believed it. I hate when someone does something to you and says sorry, and then think you are supposed to just move on like nothing ever happened. Mel knew cheating on me would hurt me and he knew it was wrong, but he did it anyway. I am sure if he was not caught, he would have kept doing it. I am sure it was enjoyable at the time. All that fun had long-lasting consequences. Meaning: DO NOT do shit to me and think I will forgive and forget that you fucked me over. I will get you back somehow. You may never find out. It may be in a big or small way. I will get the last laugh even if it takes years. Now I warn people early about how I feel about my truth. I encourage people to not hurt me because I was very revengeful.

One thing Mel taught me was that I had the power to get whatever I wanted, especially from a man. So, it was time for me to listen to his advice. First, it started with little flirting, long conversations, and office visits with Sgt Robins. I was so scared, but I had to do what I had to do. I was afraid of getting caught, getting judged, or getting kicked out of the Navy. I had worked so hard to get where I was. I knew exactly what I was doing and had no shame at this time. I started taking risks and I learned a thing or two about revenge. I used it to get what I wanted. I had a choice to get revenge or be a good girl. I do not want to be the good girl anymore. *But WHY do I have to be the one getting hurt all the time?*

Oh, it's ready to get interesting. One day I needed something bad and there was no other way for me to get it other than by asking. I was scared to shits but I had to. I became brave and asked Sgt. Robins if I could talk to him in private. I asked him if I could take a shower because I was bleeding heavily. My monthly cycles were heavy and stayed on for about seven days. I hated it and I hated that I could not shower when I wanted to. His facial expressions showed that he understood what I was going through or he liked what he saw. Which was me.

I was shocked. I did not think I was a pretty girl. He seemed to have had a great personality when he wasn't doing his job. He told me to wait until dark to shower. He then said "you can keep a secret right? Everything stays between us, right? I said, *Yes Sir, I can.* I gave him the million-dollar smile and once he smiled back that's when I knew he wanted something from me. I thought to myself, *Oh I could keep a secret. The secret should be my middle name because I had so many of them.* I would only hate to keep this secret from Blackman, my new best friend.

I was now 21 and considered myself a grown woman. Sgt. Robin was in his late thirties. We both knew what we were doing. The question was *who's more knowledgeable?* him or I. I saw his behavior change towards me. He started smiling at me often. I stayed quiet because I knew my place. He showed favoritism towards me. I was able to do more. Some people became upset and wondered why "Hargrove" gets to do this or that. He wanted to fuck me, and I knew it. His dick got hard every time I walked into his office. I knew at some point sex would come into play with us. Sex seemed to be what men wanted in the end.

Most men are only nice and do nice things for you when they want something in return. Or should I say expect something in return? It may not be today or tomorrow, but they expect something in return. Please believe this. NOTHING IS FREE!! NOTHING!! To answer all your questions. Yes! we ended up fucking on the compound of basic training. I know everyone is saying *how the fuck were you able to do that?* It was pretty easy. When everyone was asleep or when no one was there at all. First off this could not have been his first rodeo.

I was so freaking scared I did not know what to do. It started with just a kiss here and a kiss there and I guess he got extra excited from the kisses. He wanted so much more. There was an empty barracks next door, and no one was there. He asked me to meet him there to have sex. At first, it seems like a fuck for luck. Meaning I fuck you and you just be nice to me. I received favors, food, and special treatment you know. We created a tough situation for ourselves. It was hard to keep doing this secretly. So, every chance to be together was a quickie.

Whenever Robin wanted to fuck, he placed Blackman to stand watch. He waited until everyone was asleep. She still had no clue what was going on. So, I sneaked over to the next empty barracks to fuck. Yes. I said it to fuck. The first time we went there it was quick but *OK*. I waited for him there and he grabbed me from behind. He scared the fuck out of me. I said softly to him, *I've been waiting forever for this,* and he kissed me. I don't know if I really liked kissing him or if it just seemed like it was something that I had to do. I quickly pulled down my pants and my pussy was already wet and tight. It didn't take much for me to get ready. Then he gave me a few strokes and that was it! I liked a little penetration. Especially if it was big. He satisfied me.

Did I feel guilty? *Yes* and *No.* I felt bad but at twenty-one, I didn't care two shits about whose feelings I was hurting. In my head, I had been fucked over by Mel already and now it was my turn. He never really talked to me or explained himself about his ex. He said he didn't have to. So, do I owe an explanation for the naughty shit I've been doing? *No! Again, I am following his lead!* I had just enough time to shower; three minutes to be exact and go to the PX (the PX was the military store that had everything: food, clothes, electronics, alcohol, etc.) to get me something to eat and get snacks. I couldn't get shit to cook. It was only crap like tuna, Vienna sausages, saltine crackers, and chips. The easy stuff.

At some point, I had to tell Blackman. She was my best and only friend. I had two bitches stalking and hating the fact that I was doing what I wanted. We found out that one of their family members was a lieutenant or captain. They had no reason to be mad at me because they were getting away with a lot of shit way before me. Without all the fucking, I guess. At this point, I had to tell my best friend my secret. She was a smart-ass New Yorker and she kept asking me questions. I could not keep up with the lies. She kept me on my toes. One day she asked "girl how the fuck do we keep being able to walk to the PX when we want to? She then said confusingly, "something is not right." All I could do was smile and laugh.

I confessed I told her that Sgt. Robin and I were kissing, hugging, and fucking from time to time. We fucked in his office, in the empty barracks rooms, the bathroom, and anywhere we could get away. We only fucked in the wee hours of the morning. She had to promise to keep my secret. She promised and I trusted her. She was my best friend and secret holder. At first, she did not believe me. I had to prove it to her, and it took a lot of proving with her ass. She was a tough wildfire and a hard bargain. I told her about the perks I was receiving. Now everything was coming back to her. It started with being able to shower when I wanted. One night I woke her up and said we are about to shower for as long as we want. Shitttttt that was like the lottery around that motherfucker. Showering for longer than three minutes was a luxury. She still needed more convincing it wasn't enough for this hot head. It seemed like she wanted to make sure. I told her about the times we were allowed to go to PX. I told him I needed to go to the PX, and I was going with Blackman. He said "OK" and gave us the rules. We went on our way. She said, "Bitch I was wondering why we were able to go to the PX so much." Then she started teaching me that New York shit on running it up and not being so shy or scared about it.

Confessing this secret was a plus for me because now Blackman was our cover-up for every time we fucked. We stood up to fuck or fucked in the office chair. There were no beds. Sometimes it was tricky because people came in and out. It rarely happened though. Robin ran his shit, and no one was able to even knock on his door without permission. He had to protect his secret and that secret was me. But at this point, I had to tell him everything. I told him that I told Blackman because she was helping us keep our secret. She made sure no one would run up on us. At first, Sgt. Robin was a little skeptical about it because he was nervous. We both were and it was normal to be scared when you were doing extreme wrong like we were. We would be in a lot of trouble if we were to get caught.

I thought of myself as a good girl, but I was not acting like a good girl. Deep down I knew I had to take accountability. I was becoming a bad girl and being young was not a good excuse anymore. I used my attractiveness as a tool to get what I wanted. Especially when I saw that men were using me as a tool. Mel had taught me a few things without even saying anything and Blackman taught me a whole lot more. My childhood trauma had me feeling ugly and insecure. I was weak and did whatever I needed to do to survive.

I was beginning to feel pretty. This New York shit taught me, and it was hitting me differently. Blackman schooled me about confidence, and it was working. I was tooting this thing up whenever Sgt. Robin wanted it and he loved every minute of it. We fucked every chance we could. He had a good personality, and we had a good time. If a man tried too hard or seemed lame, then I would not give him three minutes of my time. It was hard to get my attention because I was tough. Robin was different. I enjoyed our time together.

I kept snacks in my rack. Rack: It's a bed or bunk bed used for the military, it's a bed with storage space under it. We kept food and snacks hidden somewhere. I was glad when we had our rack inspection that Stg. Robin was the one to do my inspection. I always kept it clean and tight. I would be fucked if anyone else did my inspections. Later we found out that the other girls that had family as captains were allowed to leave the compound altogether. They had special privileges, and they weren't even fucking anyone. This was from what we understood to be true at this time. It was good we found out late. I had no regrets and was just having fun. I was getting what I wanted at the time and the experience taught me that I should not settle for less.

One thing Stg. Robin couldn't help us with the swimming thing. We had to do it to pass our training. We had to float for five minutes after being pushed off a 12ft diving board. Blackman and I failed. We could not fucking swim at all. I was so scared of water. I almost drowned when I was small, and no one even noticed. I was traumatized and feared water. Every time I was thrown in the water, I sunk straight to the bottom. We had to do remedial swimming classes. The navy swim team tried to teach us how to swim or should I say tread water and float. I had a fear of water. This experience kicked my fear of water by 90%. I learned to float for five minutes. I knew I had to do it, so I was determined to conquer my fear. *I need to do this. I must graduate.* I had to pass. Yes!!! Blackman and I learned to swim together. We still needed to pass the battle station part. In the battle station, we had to stay up all night for twenty-four hours and run all kinds of mazes submerged in water up to our chest.

11 weeks had passed, and I was almost finished with this Bootcamp shit. The hard part had yet to come. My son was my

motivation. I would not have made it this far without him. I thought about him all the time. I thought about it, and I knew my purpose. I could not fail him. Failing was not an option. The battle station has come, and this was going to be the hard part. I had to pass. I fell asleep a few times and almost got kicked out. There were several Recruit Division Commanders, which was the RDC helping with our final battle station, at least 20 of them. One of the RDC's sprayed my face with water when I fell asleep in the middle of the training. The RDC kept saying to me if you keep falling asleep, we will dismiss you. We were running on a live battle station, or should I say a made-up ship that was sinking. I was so scared, tired, and ready for this to be over. I was cold, shaking, and crying. I just want to go home!!

Yay!!! We passed and were ready for the next level. We did it! It was time for us to graduate. I can tell you that the only way I made it through Bootcamp was by thinking of my son. Thinking about our future was the motivation that I needed to get through. I knew if I made it through this, I could get through anything. ANYTHING!! You already know Sgt. Robin had to hit it one more time. He knew he probably would never see me again. Goodbye Chicago Illinois.

CHAPTER 7

The Dirty D

Whoop whoop I was so glad that Bootcamp was over. We had a great graduation. My friends and family drove from the other side of the world to celebrate with me, and I was extra excited. Mom and Mel drove twenty-four hours to see me graduate. I felt that Mel really cared for me, but it may be too late. Mel and I were able to go to the room and hang with our family. We went out to eat and enjoyed ourselves. But I could not leave just yet. I had to stay for the Seaman Apprenticeship program. This program option allowed us to qualify for one of the "special jobs" on the ship. To me, it was a class to train us for the deck department on the ship. Nothing special about the training because I was drunk almost every day.

Mel and I did sneak away and fucked. It was pretty good, but I just didn't feel the spark anymore. The way I felt about him was not there like before and it's only because of what he did. I think at this moment I learned something about myself. I had grown up. Once I was fucked over more than once, I will lose feelings on purpose. I also stop caring about their feelings. Do not cheat on me or put some other hoe before me it makes me feel less than a woman. I felt fire in me, and I want you to feel what I feel. Don't ever make me look stupid in front of anyone, especially another woman or man. I did not put shit past no human at this time. I will snatch a soul quick when you play with my feelings. Don't let this little sweet molly maid look fool you and do not take me for granted. Mel and I kicked it until I went to my first duty station.

After the Seaman apprenticeship program, I was able to go back home to Kinston, North Carolina. I walked into Mom's house and there were dozens of roses everywhere. I said, *Mom, where did these come from?* I thought oh yea, Mel was stepping his game up. I smiled and was happy. I was like let me call him and thank him. Mom looked at me all weird and said "oh these aren't from no Mel. What your hot ass done did." I said *I didn't do anything Ma.* She said, "you are a Hargrove and I know you did something. Who is Robin Fee?" My eyes grew big, and I started smiling. Yes. The roses were from Robin. I was shocked that he took the time to even send me anything. I guess he enjoyed our fling more than I thought. He made me feel like I was worthy. He made me feel special. I deserved more and I deserved to be happy. I knew that there was someone out there for me that would treat me like a queen.

In September 2001, I was instructed to report to the United States Ship (USS) Detroit. *And guess who is on the same ship with me?* YES!!

Blackman. I jumped for joy when I saw her. I was glad that I was not alone. I did not want to make new friends. I knew we were about to raise hell on board the Dirty D. They made this mistake for this ship. Our relationship was great, and we were inseparable. We were best friends. Everyone back in Chicago knew that.

It was time for us to go to Fort Monmouth Army Base in Earl, New Jersey. We had to go through a gate and had to wait on the bus to take us from one side of the pier to the other to get to the ship. It was about five miles away due to the ship being an oiler. It seemed like it took forever for us to get from the gate to the pier. I was scared out of my mind. I had to meet a whole group of new people. Oh, and dislike a whole new group of chicks that were not going to like me. I seemed to have had a problem with the next bitch not liking me. It was so weird because it was not my problem that people could not stop their man from looking at or wanting someone else.

Well, lookie here, this ship was a meat market of men. Oh WOW! So many sexy men and women from all over the world. At least at the time, I thought they were. Side Note: Guys in uniform look so sexy. The uniform makes them look good and desirable. But let me tell you most men that wear a uniform are so lame. Outside of that uniform they are lame and were nobody special. Especially when they had rank. I also learned that you don't judge a person on looks. What looks good is not always good for you.

The first person I met was Ensign Smith. He was a cool-ass young white officer. He asked me a few questions. I told him I had a son and he asked if I was getting money for him. I was so dumb-founded like *what money?* I wasn't receiving any money for my son. I wondered why no one told me about this in the beginning. Ensign

Smith proved to me that he was smart as hell and helpful. I found out quickly that if you didn't know what's going on you will get sucked into anything. I mean anything.

Now that I know more, I want to tell anyone interested in going to the military that you should always go with someone or at least talk to someone more knowledgeable about the military. The recruiters will do anything or say anything for you to sign up to join. They can care less about helping you or discussing benefits. They do not care. I was so grateful for him helping me out because that added an extra eighteen hundred to my check. I received back pay from Bootcamp. He helped me to get right with my pay and my health insurance for my son. He also informed me that I could get housing when we dock in. But there was a catch, they will take the extra eighteen dollars for rent. That was crazy as hell.

Ensign Smith introduced me to DT1 Reed (Dental Tec). He took me to the Navy Federal Credit Union so I could get help with my paperwork to complete my new pay. DT1 Reed was a short buff dude. He was an older cat with a gold tooth and dimples. He seemed to have a nice personality and a weird laugh. He looked good in his uniform. He was head of MWR. (Moral, Welfare, and Recreation) He was responsible for handling the gym equipment, programs, games, and things to do when we hit ports. I thought he was handsome, but I was not looking for anyone at this time. I was only focused on getting my money right.

Mel warned me about the men. So, I had an idea of what to expect. Mel probably thought I wasn't listening, but I was. DT1 Reed did not come on to me or anything. He just did his job. He helped me as Mr. Smith instructed him to. I found out that the cost of living in New Jersey was high. I was happy I was getting everything situated. I would have been missing out on something I was entitled to for my child. Hell, I was already pissed about everyone getting a bonus, but not me.

My recruiter played me, and it seemed like they did it to all the kids that joined. Especially the young ones that sign up without their parents to help them with the paperwork. We were signing our life away without a clue of what was going on. All we knew was that we wanted a better life. DT1 Reed took me to my destination. I then helped him pick out gym equipment for the ship. We talked, laughed, ate, and that was it. I headed back to the ship to get things in order. I think the ship was due to go out in a few months.

The ship was old, scary, clean, and organized. We toured the ship, and it seemed as if we were walking the plank. I thought about the sharks at the bottom of the water. I felt as if they were ready to eat us alive. The females on the boat wanted us to walk back off and go home. You could see it all over their faces. As we continued to tour Officer Smith showed us the useful officers, the in-charge officers, the important officers, people in charge, or anyone who could be of any help to us. The officers showed us where we were going to sleep. It was time for us to get more comfortable. We had to share a room with over 90 other females. I thought to myself, *"yep, boot camp did prepare us for this part."*

Blackman and I went into the Navy as a Boatswain's mate and once again we had no clue what we had signed up for. We tried to find out exactly what we signed up for. I asked Ensign Smith, and he gave me the same story they gave me at MEPS which was: that you get to be like a butterfly as a Boatswain's and work with or in every department until you find one you are interested in. You can train with them after you do your time as a Boatswain's mate. Some career examples were dental tech, medical, master at arms, weapons, operation specialist, or culinary specialist. I could try them all or pick one. I found out that was a lie. As the days went on, I saw that our job was to maintain the ship. It could be a good and a bad thing. I guess I would see soon. There's no turning back now. I AM STUCK HERE!

Boatswain's mate: Cleaned the ship, dust the ship, scrub the ship, and transferred supplies and fuel from one ship to another. They also stand watch throughout the night watching for other boats, criminals, pirate ships, aliens, or whatever that may attack the ship. There were some stipulations on what you could do. Sometimes it was hard for you to train somewhere else because you were needed in that department. I had created a mindset and that was: we are just bodies and could be replaced at any time. So, try not to kill yourself trying to work for others. At first, I was pissed off about my assignment, but I later accepted it. I used it as motivation. I told myself that *I must find a career and do something with my life.*

A lot of men flirted with us. I was not interested. I was trying to be a good girl and do my time. It was funny because men were hating on the next man to make themselves look good. It was a *no for me* at that time. I smiled and kept it moving. I had conversations with them but nothing more. I had matured and was in my own world. I was an old soul. I loved to chill, play bingo, read books, and listen to music.

Blackman and I knew that we were the new meat on the ship. The men were so nice to us, and the women looked at us sideways. They started calling us Detroit Finest. We were able to get anything we wanted from them. They bought us food, pressed our uniforms, and gave us rides off base when we needed them. Blackman was still our mouthpiece. She knew what to say when to say it, how to say it, and who to say it to. We walked around like we were the shit because we felt like we were. We were beautiful women. We had nice, petite, and sexy shapes. We had nice hair, nice fat butts, and we took no shit from anybody. Blackman was much more confident. My childhood trauma played a factor in my confidence, but I was beginning to change. I felt better about myself. My best friend was working with me on my confidence.

On September 11, 2001, we were doing our 2nd day of the tour just like any other day. This day was different because we saw some stuff on the news about the war. Something was blowing up. Yes, the news! I never watched the news except for when I knew what I was looking for. I was young and the news did not interest me. It did on this day! We were touring on top of the ship and suddenly, we heard a BOOM and we saw a lot of smoke. We were in Earl, New Jersey and this is near Fort Monmouth Army Base. We were close to New York and close enough to see New York from the ship across the water. *Oh My! We just witnessed a plane hitting the twin towers in New York.* Smoke was everywhere!! We all were clueless about what the hell was going on. I went into the military thinking I would never go to War. Damn...

I was shocked and scared because I never thought the war would happen while I was in the Navy. I did not think I would have to fight or deal with weapons. That was a lie!!!! I had to get suited and booted quickly. They quickly announced that we were officially at war and were ordered to pull out to sea. All we heard were sirens and horns blowing and the captain spoke about us pulling out to sea and having us report to our duty station. We all only had a little time. We had less than 24 hours to get things in order with our families and get the necessary things needed for our departure. Our ship could be a target because it was an oiler. An oiler could take out a whole city if blown up. We didn't have much time. We had to prepare to be away for at least six months or more. We needed to get our affairs and families in order. I called my mother and told her what was going on and asked her to take care of Donny. She had the power of attorney over my son so there was not much for me to do to get my affairs in order. I had to do that before I joined. Our Bosin Scott quickly said, "Do not expect to come back anytime soon." That sent me into tears. WE WERE AT WAR!!!! FUCK ME!! I WAS PISSED AND SCARED TO DEATH!! I didn't think the ship would go anywhere; let alone go to War.

I called my mom crying like a baby. I wanted to go home. I wanted all the prayers and love I could get from Mom. I felt power in her prayers. I had no choice but to put my big girl panties on. Out to sea, I went. The ship experience felt like we were in a small city. Everything we needed was on it. We had a gym, barbershop, kitchen, dentist, medical department, laundromat, police department, drivers, cleaners, helicopters, engineer room, freezers, televisions, computer stations, and more. However, it was not a cruise ship kind of city. It was more like a third-world country city. Everything was routine and scheduled just like the military you watched on television.

Our job as a Boatswain's mate consisted of us being responsible for sailing, rigging, anchoring the ship, and cordage dealing with cords and ropes. We cleaned the ship every day. We painted, dusted, or any other thing our superiors wanted or could find for us to do. We were also the ones to do the VERTRAP: Vertical replenishment, UNREP: Underway replenishment, and RAS: Replenishment at sea. These were ways to send supplies, fuel, food, water, and mail from one ship to another, which was the most important job to most on the ship. We all were always waiting for mail so getting mail was the best thing ever!!!

I thought we didn't do much of anything but as you can see, our job was important. We were considered in the Deck department, and it seemed as if we were ranked at the bottom. The deck department is responsible for driving and operating the ship, while at sea and in port. The deck department wears many hats. I found our job interesting at times. We never slept over five hours. There was always something to do. The job was boring but fun at the same time. Some days we had activities to do and some days we chilled. Chilling was rare because they made sure they worked the shit out of us when they could. There were times that we were so busy and had to just shower and sleep. We were painters, cleaners, primers, divers, scrubbers, and firefighters, we were whatever they needed us for to maintain this ship. A lot of times we were just going with the flow because we didn't know what the hell we were doing. I learned something new every day. The experience was so new to me and exciting at the same time.

We had time to ourselves too. We worked out and pampered ourselves. Blackman and I smoked cigarettes on the back of the ship. It was so freaking dark on the stern of the ship. I mean pitch dark! It was the type of dark in which you could not see your hands. We had been on the ship for about a week, and I started feeling bad. I was not feeling well from the waist down if you know what I mean. I was discharging. I never discharged or had any issues down there. I wanted to know what was going on. So, I decided to go to the doctor to get checked. Side note: when you go to medical school everyone will learn your business eventually.

Well, you would think that your information would be con-fidential. Sadly, this was not so. The same people that worked there are just like you and me. They had access to our records, and they all were in training, so they didn't know any better. Some people were afraid to see the doctor because they did not want their business all over the ship. Anyway, I didn't know the rules and I thought doctors and nurses would keep your information safe. NOT!!! I never dis-charged before, so I was scared as hell. I began to have so many awful thoughts. Something was wrong with my fatty patty. I fucked Sgt. Robin but that never happened the entire time we were together and besides, he wore protection. Sgt. Robin was extra careful. He knew that we could not explain a pregnancy in Bootcamp.

I had been with Mel last, so I knew it was him. I needed to know what was going on with my precious fatty patty. The doctor came in and told me I had Trichomonas WHICH WAS A FUCK-ING STD!!! Of course, I went to look it up to see where the fuck it came from. I felt stupid all over again. I knew right then he had to go! I could not deal with him anymore. Me going away was the best thing ever. I guess I had to take some of the responsibility. It could have been me. It was unlikely. I was fucking around with Sgt. Robin and Mel. I explained it to the doctor, and he said he thought it came from the last person I had sex with. Which was Mel.

I had not had sex with Sgt. Robin in two months. Either way, I was mad at Mel and myself. I talked to Mel and at some point, we spoke on it. I remember we fussed, and of course, he had his theory about the situation as always. He was so cocky and felt as if he could do whatever he wanted. He was a smooth talker, and it showed every time he talked. This was the story he told me: He said that the STD came from us having anal sex. He said something about the transfer of bacteria and feces. We did have anal sex a few times. I didn't know what to believe. I took my medication and moved in silence because I knew I had done some wrong shit too. I knew that Sgt. Robin and I used condoms all the time. Mel and I raw dogged all the time. We had nasty sex. No matter where I got the STD from, I decided to stop fucking with him. It was time for me to move on. I did not trust him.

I had always been independent, and I went to the doctor on a regular. I had to learn how to take care of myself on my own at an early age. My Godmother Tessa taught me about good hygiene and to want more out of life. She will always be special to me because she saved my life. I went to the doctor as a young girl often because I had Medicaid, and it was free. I walked to the doctor's office whenever I needed to. As early as fourteen. If I felt an itch, smell, or anything I would walk to the doctor. Nevertheless, I had to focus. We were at war.

America was under attack, and this was something serious. I was scared shitless. All I could think about was getting home. But as the days went on the days seemed normal. It seemed as if we were just cruising around the world. We had a lot of training to prepare us for this possibility, but everything was like a normal day. One of the scariest moments on the ship was when one of the boilers blew up on the ship and everyone thought the ship was going to sink. There was a huge hole that made us think we were going to die. We were equipped. We went through scary moments throughout the eight months, but the crew maintained everything. Overall, the crew kept us calm throughout the war. We even had some fun. We played bingo and had barbecues. We still had our extensive training. We were able to make phone calls, use the computers to email, and we worked out to keep fit.

CHAPTER 8

I'm a Single Girl Now

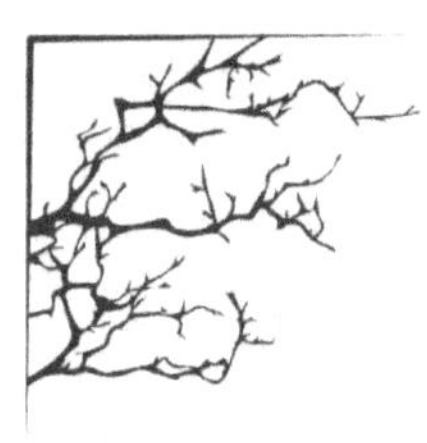

My time with Mel had run its course. It was good while it lasted, and I do not regret being in a relationship with him. He was older and more experienced. I just went with whatever I thought would keep him and make him happy. *I mean isn't that what I was supposed to do for my man?* Our experience together was a lesson learned and I learned a lot from him. A LOT!!! After dealing with Mel, I was very observant of my surroundings. I started giving warnings to people in my life.

I told my friends, my family, my coworkers, and anybody *"DO NOT FUCK ME OVER OR DO SHIT TO ME THAT YOU DO NOT WANT TO BE DONE TO YOU. I DO NOT FORGET AND I CAN BE REVENGEFUL"* I still tell people this up until this day. I knew it was over. I never went backward in a relationship or a friendship. Especially if I was hurt, made a fool of, betrayed, lied on, lied to, unfaithful, disloyal, deception, backstab, or wronged in any way. I do not like it. I take it to heart, and I have learned that it is up to me to deal with it. And I chose NOT TO!!!

We saw the same people every day and ate the same food every week. The food was not good at all, but it worked for the time being. The ship was huge. We had to learn our way around. I was not good with directions and got lost often. I look up and I see DT1 Reed. I remembered him because he was the gentleman that helped me with my paperwork. He flirted with me. I was not impressed because I had heard that he was interested in every girl that came on the ship. He seemed to not prefer looks or body type. Both the ladies and guys on the ship told us stories about Reed. Someone told us that there was a bet on all of us new girls. The bet was to see who hit it first meaning who fuck the new chick first.

We were young and thought we knew everything. We did not know squat. Hell, we may have been running our catch that nigga game. Blackman and I were headhunter investigators. We were on a mission to figure out who was who, what was what, and who was going to be our boo thang while we were here. We both wanted a boo thang to chill with while we were out to sea. I was still a little shy and scared of everything. Blackman on the other hand spoke for me most of the time. She knew what to say and when to say it. She knew how to get what she wanted or needed.

I was a young woman and I had sexual needs. I had never been away from home and had always been in a relationship. My fatty patty was getting a little lonely. Two long months had passed and every nigga on the ship started to look like Denzel Washington, Morris Chestnut, Nas, Shemar Moore, The Rock, or any sexy nigga. In reality that was not what was there. It was just men that looked kinda sort of good in uniform. The uniforms looked good.

In my eyes Reed was nice. He was nice looking. He had a nice body, a nice smile, quiet, and reserved. Blackman told Reed that I wanted an "appointment" and it was not a dental appointment. It was a what's up with them drawers' appointment. My shyness was embarrassing. I was glad that I had Blackman on my side. Blackman was straightforward and said what was on her mind. I went along with her plan. I was interested in Reed, but I wanted to go slow. I usually did not take risks, but I did. I DID IT!

I made an appointment with him at midnight the next day. I was scared to death. What was I getting myself into? I needed some excitement in my life. I took a shower, put lotion on, shaved my fatty patty, and brushed my teeth. Thoughts of getting caught started running through my mind. I was extra scared. We were not supposed to have sex on the ship. I knew where this was going, and fucking was at the end of the tunnel. I was about to break the rules. I figured that other people were doing the same thing. If the door was locked and keys were only available for certain people: then more than likely they were fucking behind closed doors. I knew people were fucking on the ship no matter who denied it. I felt as if everyone had somebody on the ship.

So, it was time, Midnight had come, and I was ready for my appointment. We sat and talked for two to three hours and learned a few things about one another. Yes, and then we did it. The first time we had sex was a quickie because we both were scared that someone could walk in. He sat me on the dental counter and ate my pussy. He was a different pussy eater. It seemed as if he tried to figure out the pussy to make me cum. I liked that. He then bent me over and gave me life. It was so good. But I couldn't enjoy it as I wanted to because I was scared and nervous. He didn't seem nervous at all. He must have done this before. I went back to my rack and listened to Alicia Keys which I listened to every night. I had a huge smile on my face. It felt good to know that someone wanted me.

The next day I went back for a new appointment. As soon as I walked in the door, he was all over me. He kissed and caressed me, and this turned me on to my core. I was ready! He sat me on the counter and before I knew it my underwear was on the floor. He ate my pussy, and it was great. I threw my head back and enjoyed the feeling of him eating my pussy. My pussy was throbbing and creaming. It scared me because I squirted, and it felt amazing. I could feel his excitement. He was so excited he had this chance to feel inside me. He grabbed my neck and threw his head back in excitement. He was biting his bottom lip and it turned me on. He was working with a nice size. I wanted to feel every inch, every stroke, and every thrust. It did not last long but we both got exactly what we wanted, a NUTT! It was great!!

Afterward, we looked at one another and laughed. I was still scared someone would walk in. It was unlikely because the door was locked, and a chair was behind the door. I think he and the other tech Gonga had an agreement because Gonga had a girl too. I know they were fucking. Reed and Gonga kept each other secrets. None of what they were doing could get back to the big boss. Doctor Venter was Reed's and Gonga's, supervisor. He was the Chief Officer of the dental office and was a nerdy, dingy, corny, and weird white officer. All in all, he was a good funny guy. However, he had the power to strip both Reed and Gonga from their positions. Therefore, it was important for them to have each other's back.

Reed and I were in a secret relationship on the ship, and we kept it just that. A secret. When the ship pulled back in from war. Reed and I spent a lot of time getting to know one another. Yes! we fucked the entire time on the ship. He was hooked and so was I. But you know most men will not show how much they care. I later found out that he was married. Of course, he gave me this story of what was going on. He said they were separated and will be getting a divorce soon. He said he caught her cheating, and she was cheating with another military guy. He dogged her out as if she was the reason why they were getting a divorce. Oh, it gets worse. Reed said that she cheated with his good friend. I believed him. I thought he was genuinely telling the truth.

A few days later I heard he had a baby with a girl who had been on the ship. This supposedly was the reason why she left. He said she was crazy and how she had an orgy with a lot of guys. According to him, she doesn't know who the daddy was and that she was married. So, to answer your question, yes, he was a part of the alleged orgy. So, one day his alleged baby momma came on the ship when we pulled in. She made it her business to bring the baby on the ship. I felt the stares and knew that they were talking about me. I did not care. He said the baby was not his and I believed him. I knew he was not liked on the ship. I had heard so many rumors about him the whole time we were out to sea. It seemed to come from every guy that wanted to talk to me and every girl that hated me. I trusted my man and waited for whatever came next.

Phillip came on the ship with her baby. Phillip spoke Spanish so I assumed that she was a Latino. She looked like a scrubby old white lady. She was short, maybe 5ft 4in tall. She had a small frame, big tits, fair skin, rosy cheeks, fine dark bob-length hair, and she wore glasses. She looked like she might have had a skin condition. She was not attractive to me at all. But to each his own. Her baby looked bi-racial. He looked African American and Latino in complexion. As soon as I saw the baby, I looked at Reed and said, *I hate to burst your bubble, but that baby is yours he looks just like you.* Phillip looked at me in disgust. I am sure one of her friends on the ship informed her about Reed and me. Reed was with me, and everyone knew it. It was no longer a secret. I did not care what anyone said or heard. I did not care at all. Reed was my man, and I was going to trail his way.

I am not sure what Phillip's motive was in bringing her baby on the ship. Whatever it was, it did not change shit. I saw that the baby looked like it could be his child. I wasn't shocked because I heard the shit the entire cruise. I already knew it was a possibility. The disappointment was really; how did you choose this woman to fuck? She was loud, rude, and feisty. I guess she thought if she was loud, I would fear her. That was not the case at all. She was not worth my time. Whatever they had going on was not my business. To be honest, they both were married, and both were in the wrong. I was not there when they fucked and made the baby, nor do I have to help to take care of the baby. She was not the cutest in the bunch and her attitude did not match it either. She hated my ass for no reason.

Reed and I had so much fun together. I took chances with him. We drove to North Carolina to see my family. We stopped at rest stops to have sex and it was hot and heavy. Yes, it began with me on top and it ended with me on top. One time we were brave enough to stand outside the car and I let him hit it from the back. It felt so freaking good. The challenge, the excitement, the danger, the adrenalin, and the fucking goodness were worth it all. The police caught our ass one time and scared the shit out of me. It still was good, and he knew exactly what we were doing because the windows were fogged up.

It was time to spice our relationship up a little. Reed and some of the head officers hung out together and we had too many drinks. They were much older. They were in their 50's and acted like rednecks. I didn't judge and it seemed they didn't either. We took shots of Tequila, and we all were drunk as crap. The table was filled up with tequila shots. Over 50 shots were lined up all over the table. We took shots after shot. Herd, Smith, Reed, and I ended up at the hotel with the heart-shaped tub. The popular hour hotel called Hot Tub hotel was at the corner of the ship dock. Everybody went there to fuck. This was the beginning of me being with women. We had a foursome, and it was so weird and memorable. We were so fucked up. I do not remember how we got there.

This was the first time I ate pussy without being forced to. I liked it and enjoyed it. It was a whole different feeling. I loved rubbing and touching a soft woman. She smelled and looked good. Watching her bite her lip turned me on. She acknowledges how good she felt, and I could tell she liked what I was doing to her. On the other hand, it was the total opposite when being with a man. A man hides everything. Most of the time we do not know how they feel. Most men act as if they are scared to moan. They hold everything inside. Everything was rough about a man. A man's hand, feet, and everything were rough.

Well, I ate pussy and loved it. So, Reed would be doing the fucking and I would eat their pussy. We changed positions and persons so many times. It was exciting but weird at the same time. This is how it went down. Reed fucked Herd and then Smith. Herd did not like the penetration and that was fine because we switched up again. Reed penetrated Smith while I ate Herd's pussy. Then Reed fucked me, and I ate Smith's pussy. Smith ate Herd's pussy and then everyone at my pussy. It was very interesting and very different. A bunch of fucking. Yes! We used protection when we fucked. This was our special secret. *What an amazing experience.* We did not speak of this ever again. That "special" sexual experience changed my life forever.

I now had a high interest in women. But I would never approach a woman at all.

The only way I connected with women sexually was through Reed or if they came on to me. It seemed that women were afraid to approach me for some reason. (They just didn't know that I would suck the pussy until the end of the week with no complaining) I was so serious.

Reed made me feel a little more comfortable about our relationship when he took me to Maryland to meet his wife and kids. I know it sounds weird, but it was what it was. She was cordial and nice. I could tell that she was in her feelings. She was a little bitter. If I were in her shoes, I would be too. She started throwing shade toward Reed. She told me all kinds of shit to scare me off. She told me he cheated and did not take care of his children. She was acting like a mom warning her child. But who do you think I was supposed to believe? Him or her? I believed him because he was brave enough to show me off and let her know I was his girl. I thought he was doing the right thing. I wanted to see for myself. I was tired of hearing the rumors.

Reed and I spent a lot of time together. The ship needed a lot of maintenance, so we were docked at the shipyards. The ship had its regular maintenance and repairs done there. It was in Philadelphia, Pennsylvania. (Philly) The military gave us housing at the barracks. We were not allowed to live on the ship while the ship was being repaired. We woke up every morning to help clean, fix, and prepare the ship for our next tour. I noticed Reed flirting with other girls.

I had had enough at this point! He thought I was stupid and did not know who he was dealing with. He had inappropriate conversations with other girls. So, I, with my revengeful self, started having my conversations. One day when I was visiting Mom, I bumped into Mel. We exchanged numbers. I did not care about Reed's feelings. I felt something was going on with him. I realized he was a piece of shit, and I knew it. I still loved him, and I knew he loved me. I found out he was talking to some girl named Pam who lived in New Jersey. My eyes were open but not enough to just leave him.

My nose started bleeding while I was at the shipyards. It would not stop. Everyone around me thought something was wrong because there was blood everywhere. The doctor asked me to tilt my head back, and when I did blood started gushing out of my mouth. The crew knew how Reed felt about me after that day. He rode in the ambulance to the hospital. He was so scared. Hell, I was scared. The doctors did not have any explanations for why my nose would not stop bleeding. She said something was wrong with my blood count. I never followed up on it. Later that night I found a message on his phone. He was fucking a girl name Pam in New Jersey again. I was so pissed. I kept my cool and we went out to eat at a restaurant called Fat Tuesday. They also sold frozen drinks that I liked. It gets me drunk every time. On the way home, we got in an altercation in the middle of the road. I was drunk. I woke up the next day and he had two blackeyes. I asked him *How did you get that?"*

He said "oh you did this" I looked confused and whispered out loud to myself, *What the hell did I do?* He explained the fight and I was shocked and embarrassed.

CHAPTER 9

The Russian Girl

Six months had passed, and we had a barge connected to the ship. A barge is a small floating boat for housing people who were doing construction on the ship. Yes! I was finally able to change my job description. I was a culinary specialist. I had converted over to a chef on the ship, so I worked in the galley which is also known as a large kitchen. This was directly across from the dental office where Reed worked. There was a new girl on the scene. She was a Russian girl named June. June was a very small lady. She was 4ft 8in tall. She had a manly-looking face and a long nose like a witch. She weighed about 100lbs. She had crooked teeth and a weird, shaped mouth. Her mouth looked like it was sunk in. She was older than we were, and she was fit. She looked like a yoga instructor. She walked around the ship with tights and no panties. She had most of the men on the ship going crazy over her. This was not surprising because most men look at the body and not the face.

The ship was a game and Reed kept playing the game. It seemed to me that he wanted to be the first to hit the new girl. *Why are men so greedy when they have what they need?* They have something good and still want to play. WHY? Well, Reed won the bet because he hit her first. She came to me asking too many questions about us. That was suspicious enough for me to believe it was true. Remember, we are not allowed to have relationships on the ship. So, whenever someone asked me if Reed and I were together the answer was always no. June kept asking and I told her to mind her fucking business. She was pissed the fuck off. I also did not want him to get in any trouble because of her.

He fucked up! The rumors came out that he fucked her, and she found out about me. She did not like that. She came to me while I was in the shower butt booty naked soaping, and I was thinking about getting my pussy eaten that night. Shitttt, she opened my shower curtain and said, "you are lying bitch you lied about Reed." I tried to get to her ass, but someone came in between us, so we didn't fight. I told her if she didn't get the fuck out of my face, we will have a whole new problem. I told her she was disrespectful. She came to me and said, "if you do not believe me, I will record him." So, I went and bought a recorder for her to record him. I knew she was telling the truth.

Reed was not stupid. Her plan did not work because when she tried to record him, he did not say anything that suggested they had been intimate. He told her to go away and that he did not know what she was talking about. He said one thing that stood out and the most important words in my eyes. He said, "nothing is going on between us." That only made her madder at him. As a woman who had been hurt, I understood her pain. She thought he liked her. But after he fucked her, he disowned her. I knew that she was not the one to fuck with. It was about to go down and he deserved everything that was coming to him. Yes, he broke some of the rules by having sex on the ship. Hell, everyone was having sex on the ship. Let's just say that nobody's husband or wife is safe aboard a Navy ship. June took shipmate to a whole new level. When you are in a situation like this, the best thing is to just keep your dick in your pants until you are in a better environment.

Reed had just made Chief and of course, EVERYONE was upset about it. No one liked him. He was cocky and he mostly got what he wanted. Almost everyone was against him. I believe they hated the confidence he had in himself. He even had strangers disliking him. Chief Reed had made himself a new enemy. June placed him on sexual harassment charges. Eventually, we knew Reed would pay for the shit he did to women on the ship. June would be the girl that put the icing on the cake for his ass. He had to go to Captain's Mast which is like a court trial with the captain. June told everything and of course, Reed denied it and she brought me into it. She asked me to tell the court that we were fucking to get her point across. I said NO *bitch I am not snitching I did what I did because I wanted to. I am not here to get anybody in trouble.* She even told them about the recorder incident.

The officers and the Master at arms "police" did search my rack to look for the recorder. You know I was smarter than that. I had someone hide it for me. I denied everything she said about me. I was ready to fight her because she was trying to get me in trouble as well.

I was so mad the Navy Police had to contain me and shut me up. I lied for Reed to save him and his career. I did not want him to get in any more trouble. He looked sad and hurt after this day.

Another chief on the ship by the name of Chief Rich was trying to calm me down because I was going the fuck off. She told too many lies. I said to myself *If I was going to get kicked out of the military because of her; I may as well beat her ass right here.* I never saw Chief Reed tear up, but I could tell he wanted to cry. He knew he had fucked up his career. All for a piece of ass. I was thinking to myself, your *hoe days should be over after this.* Maybe this was the lesson he needed. All of this happened right before we were to pull out for a three to fourth-month tour. He was stripped back down to 1st class meaning they took Chief from him. He was released from the ship and forced to retire. June was released from the ship as well for her safety. There were a few people mad at her for what she did.

It was time for us to get underway again. Reed and I were supposedly still together. I decided to stick by him. I called Reed two weeks after the ship pulled out to sea. I listened to his messages and guess who left a message? Pam! I never met Pam. He told me she was a civilian he met before we got on the ship. She lived in New Jersey. Oh my God and What the fuck! I am thinking to myself that he *just will not learn and that is cool*! DO NOT fuck me over or make me look bad. You will not get away with it. We started communicating by email. I loved him and thought we had something special. I knew the games had to stop. There were limited computers to use on the ship and the dental office was taken over by a whole new crew. I used the computer in Chief Rich's office to email Reed as often as I could. Our email chats became smaller and smaller. However, he did send me care packages. He sent me huge XL underwear and shit. Only because he thought I was still over 200lbs.

I went into a deep depression after this and started working out. I mean my workout journey was intense. I went from 220 pounds to 140 pounds. I needed to get back focused on myself and my son. I did just that. I cooked myself wonderful healthy meals. I started taking care of myself. Chief Rich checked on me a lot. We started to create a nice friendship. He helped me with working out. I fixed special snacks and meals for him. We both were trying to do better with our health and body.

The food I had to prepare on the ship was not seasoned and was not good. It was bland. So, I tried new recipes. I baked food, fried fish, and tuna salad. I was the food queen on the ship. I made it into soul food. I was breaking the rules. I was supposed to stick to their recipes. I was limited on what I could cook. However, I still made some nice and interesting things. Well in my eyes Reed was still considered my man and he made sure I knew that. He sent me care packages every two weeks, he emailed me often, and he emailed other people on the ship to check on me.

I was now back focused on myself. All it took was him leaving me out for the wolves. We were still a couple, but I decided to do what I wanted. I felt as if I was the only woman Reed cared for. I felt like we had something special. I believe people wondered to themselves "damn what she has to get him like this." It seemed as if I would continue to put up with his bull until we forcefully separated or moved apart. Oh my, this seemed very familiar. Was I acting like my mom? Mom did it when I was a child. She moved away and we became homeless many times. All because she was getting away from a man. I hope this will not be my pattern.

Rich and I communicated every day. I enjoyed our conversations. We became friends. I talked about Reed a lot to him. I was still stuck on Reed. I learned a lot. Chief Rich said he was unaware of our relationship because Reed never told him. He also disclosed some things that Reed did behind my back. He had sex with June, Richardson, Kennedy, Chance, Phillip, and Mully. Reed and Rich talked about certain girls together, but he totally denied me. I felt that Reed was a snake, and nothing surprised me. I fell hard for him, and I was in denial about a lot of things that were right in my face.

Rich and I became close, and we spent a lot of time together. One day I said to him *you are lucky*. Rich looked at me puzzled and said "why do you say that" I told him *you are lucky because you and Reed are friends or best friends*. He said, "clearly we are not best friends and if we were he would have told me that you guys were dating." I thought to myself, well *he may have a point*. He never told Rich that we were a couple. He denied it. He told him about the other bitches he was fucking on and off the ship. (It's funny how now that I have gotten older; I know that men will say anything to get in your panties.)

I thought they were cool but not best friends. Now that I think about it, Reed talked shit about him a lot. He was pissed about Captain's Mast and felt that Rich had a lot to do with what was going on. Chief Rich was the Police Officer on the ship. I think Chief Rich tried to warn Reed several times about June and he didn't listen. He just denied everything. Reed was a good liar and he lied about anything that made him look good or to save his ass.

CHAPTER 10

Left His Ass Crying

Rich and I became more than just friends. We did not plan for this to happen. It just happened. Rich and I started fucking two months into the deployment. Rich was kind, funny, sexy, and very serious. He knew he was fine, and he knew he could get what and who he wanted when he wanted. He was also loving and romantic. He was not afraid to hold hands, hug, or kiss. This was something I had been longing for. He knew what to do to win me over. I was not sure how he affected other girls, but he knew how to get me. I wanted this for a long time. I wanted to feel special. I felt him and he felt me.

It was easy for us to get in the mood. I showered and we had our nightly conversations. Our conversations turned south quickly. We started kissing, breathing heavily, rubbing, touching, and then it happened. We fucked right in his office. The door was locked.

Locked offices meant that fucking was going on. This was my second locked door. His dick was not as big as Reed's, but it was good. I rode him like a stallion, and I took control. I moaned, shook, and creamed all over the place. I grabbed the back of his head and threw my head back with every stroke. I paused so he would not cum. I needed him to not cum fast. I am sure it made it worse when he felt my pussy throbbing at the same time. His facial expressions told me that he loved every minute of it.

I had a wonderful time with him every time. He was different. He was caring. He wanted me just as much as I wanted him. He showed it from there on. I went to bed with a smile on my face. I did not sleep much because we stayed up talking and learning about one another. I knew he was married. I learned in conversation that they were on bad terms and separated. This was the story that he told me, and I believed him. He said they were not having sex. He felt that she was dealing with someone else. He was unsure if it was a man or woman. I knew that he was super unhappy with her and after that, I did not care about his wife. He had a daughter with his wife and a son with someone else who was older. Rich and Brenda, his wife, had been together for 20+ years. I did not know who the cheater was in the relationship. I did not care. I was focused on getting fucked and loved on.

After spending so much time with him I saw how cool he was, and I was down. It started with him telling me that he only had one girl to suck his dick and make him cum. I was curious to know who the girl was. I asked if she was on the ship. He replied "Yes" and of course, I was nosey. He told me her name was Chance. I said *oh ok*. He looked at me and I looked at him. I couldn't believe this older man was interested in me at all. He gave me so much more attention than Reed did. He didn't care who saw us. I am sure people knew we had a fling going on. After work, I stayed at his office until the wee hours of the morning. We had long conversations about life. I so adored him and fell for him hard. I believe the feeling was mutual.

Within the next few weeks, I told him I wanted to see if I could make him cum with my mouth. He looked shocked and smiled so hard. I told him I was serious and wanted to try. Of course, no nigga will turn down not freaking head. He locked the door and turned to me and said I'm ready. He pulled his uniform and boxers down to his ankles and sat in the chair. I pulled my hair back like I was ready to work. The temperature was cool in the room. I heard people walk by occasionally. I was nervous and turned on at the same time. He looked at me and I looked down at him biting my lip. I asked him if he wanted it and he said yessssss. I bent down to kiss him passionately. I placed a pillow on the floor, got on my knees, and rubbed my left hand on his chest. I caressed his chest with my left hand, and I used my right to play with the dick. My hand gripped his shaft, and my wet mouth covered the tip of his dick. I heard him moaning as it felt so good.

I knew I had to perform because I wanted to make him cum. I teased his head with my lips covering slobbering all over his manhood. Then I stroked and sucked at the same time. I fit his whole dick in my mouth and looked up at him at the same time. He was impressed with the mouth work. I sucked and slopped and stroked until there was an explosion in my mouth. I swallowed it all to impress him more. I had one time to perform, and I went all out. I came up wiping my face off and he kissed me as no other had. We both were speechless. He cleaned off with a towel. It was late so I left and went to sleep. I left him a little gift just to keep him in Awee.

The next day we flirted all day and every time we saw one another on the ship. All smiles!!!! Later, that night we met up again, and this time we fucked. He fucked the shit out of me. We never took our clothes off. All sexual encounters on the ship were quickies because we had to stay prepared for a door knock. He sat in the chair and sucked my pussy while I stood up. I straddled him with my dripping wet pussy and let it slide. The head going in was a pleasure for me. *Oh, how it feels so fucking good.* This nice tight pussy was all ready for it. I slid down on his dick slowly working the tip first. Then my pussy just devoured his entire dick. He was so impressed with how good it felt for him to be inside me. It didn't take long for him to explode. We kept switching positions to help him last longer. He bent me over towards the desk. I placed one leg up on the desk and he pounded my guts out. I was turned on by it so much that he had to cover my mouth. I was dripping wet, and I wanted more and more. Then BOOM he busts all inside of me. He never wore a condom.

From that day on we fucked almost every night. We did not fuck when my period was on. We pulled in six months later and I fucked Rich right before I left the ship. We were fucking fucking by then. We were loving one another. Rich was on duty and could not leave the ship.

The deployment was over. Mom, my son, and my siblings were there to watch us pull in from our six-month deployment. Reed was there also.... I was hoping that he did not show up at all. He drove from Maryland to visit. I guess he thought he was coming to claim his throne and make shit right. My mind was somewhere else. I was not thinking about his cocky ass. We all went to dinner together. Reed and I got a hotel! I believe Reed noticed that I had an "I don't care" attitude toward him. After a while, I saw how stupid I looked.

My entire attitude had changed. I lost weight and I looked good. I looked like a whole snack. Hell, I was fine.

We went to our hotel room, and I let Reed eat my pussy. Yes, after I had fucked Rich. I did not care. I thought Reed was being messy. He took me to Rich's house as if he wanted to visit his "friend." He knew damn well they were not buddy old pals. I believe someone had already told Reed that I and Rich were hanging out a lot. I was sure he did not know we were fucking. Rich and his wife were home when we stopped by. We pretended like we did not know what was going on. Reed even tried to make Rich jealous by making it seem like we were still together and in love. I was thinking to myself, *nigga if you do not get off me.*

Reed walked out of the room for a minute and Rich, and I locked eyes. I knew he wanted me right then. We could not blow our cover now. It would be too risky. His wife did not need to find out this way. Because bitter people will take you to the bank. Especially when it came to you leaving them for someone else; especially some-one much younger. On our ride home, Reed looked at me and said, "yea I just wanted to stop and see my best friend." I started laughing like shit and said *oh now you guys are best friends*? I told him to take me back to the room. I then told him it was over between us. He still didn't get it. He did not believe me and did not take me seriously. He laughed at me and told me that I was not going anywhere. I said *OK I can show you better than I can tell you.*

I was so ready to get myself a new car. I had saved just for that. Reed did not want me to get my car. Maybe he wanted to have control over me. Reed was history and I was completely over him. At this point, I only thought of myself and my son, Donny. I depended on him to take me places and that was the only way for me to get around. Reed did not live in New Jersey anymore; he was in Maryland. He had a green Montoro sport stick shift car. He never let me drive it. I did not care because I didn't like driving a stick shift. Yes, I knew how to drive a stick. I gave Reed so many chances and warnings. He planted in his head that he had this young girl under his finger. He thought I would never leave or fuck anyone else. Boy was he wrong about me! It was time for me to get my own and not depend on him for anything.

The next day I went car hunting with Reed. I wanted a Mitsubishi Eclipse so bad. We went to the dealership of course Reed was so adamant about me not getting a car of course. He finally accepted us not being together and offered to help me look for my car. We went to two dealerships, Mitsubishi, and Hyundai. I was denied to Mitsubishi. I needed a cosigner. Reed volunteered to cosign for me, but my answer was HELL NO!! I went to the Hyundai dealership instead and a nice lady named Mandy in sales helped me all the way. She connected me with First Atlantic Credit Union, and they gave me the entire loan and my payments were $486 a month. She told me to refinance in six months to a year and the interest and the payments will go down. This was great advice for me.

Yay! I drove away in my own brand new 2004 Hyundai Sonata and it had only five miles on it. I was so happy, and I felt so accomplished. I did it all on my own. I did it without my mother, father, or a man. I knew then that I could depend on myself to get things done without help from others. I had been working on my credit and my savings. Master Chief Jackson hipped me to the game of credit score and savings when I was on the ship. He told me that your credit is more important than what people took seriously. I saved a lot of money while on my cruises and put it away for emergencies. Master Chief was right about everything he told me, and I am thankful that he took the time to share knowledge with me. I drove my new shiny 4-door silver Hyundai Sonata right off the lot with the biggest smile I could ever have.

I had to report back to the ship that Tuesday morning. We only had a few days off. Mom's husband Tony B was from the New Jersey area, and they went to visit his family. Mom met me on the base. It was time for me to go back to the ship and it was time for my family to go back home. I knew Rich was waiting for me back on the ship. I was ready to see him.

I told Reed that it was over, but he did not seem to listen. He followed me everywhere trying to convince me that we were meant to be together. From the dealership to the base. He was hot on my tail. I knew and he knew it was completely over and that was that. There was no changing my mind about us being together. As we were saying our goodbyes Reed started crying and begging I mean real tears. He talked nonsense at this point. He begged for me to give him another chance. I had no more chances to give. I had given him too many chances.

I looked over at my family and I saw them crying. Donny played in the car with his cousins. He did not know what was going on. I told Mom to get on the road and that I would see them in a few weeks. I drove off while they all stayed there crying. Did I feel bad for Reed? *HELL NO!* I did not have any more energy for him. He did not care about me or my feelings when he was doing his dirt or until he got in trouble. I had enough and finally was able to put my foot down.

It took a lot for me to be done. When I am done, I AM DONE! Hell, I was over it. I gave him several chances and my mind was now on Rich. I was feeling Rich and that was where I wanted to be. After hearing all the crying and begging it was time for me to get to my man Rich. I knew he had a wife at home but when we were on the ship, he was mine. I knew he was waiting for me on the ship for some good old *wet wet*. I went straight to the ship with my new man. I missed being with him. We made a bed for the weekend. We were prepared to fuck the whole weekend. The ship was empty. He stayed on the ship with me when he was off duty. He said he didn't want to go home to the nagging wife who complained about everything. But no worries I will handle it for you, ma'am.

We fucked all night and all morning. We fell in love with one another over time and there was nothing to separate us. We were stuck like glue. I believe almost everyone knew we were together. He kept an eye on me and I kept an eye on him. He was married with children. He never wore his ring, and we did not talk about it anymore. *You are now my man.*

Blackman and I were still inseparable. We had an apartment on base. We split the bills and that was great. We had a ball there and enjoyed every minute of the time we had together. Rich came over every chance he could. We fucked every day that he came over and it was great. He rode his bike to my house and hid it in the house. It was so funny because he lived two streets over and whenever he had the chance to get away, he did. Guess who was ready for him? Me!

I was able to get Donny often now that I had my apartment. I traveled to pick him and my brother up. They stayed with me until it was time for us to get underway on the ship. Donny was my world and anything he wanted I bought for him. Donny was the reason for me making it to where I was. He was my motivation. No one or nothing came before my son. Oh my, I did not see this coming. I found out that My brother and my best friend Blackman were fucking. He was my babysitter. But I guess they decided to get busy with one another.

Blackman was very open, and she told me, and they were fucking. She did not hide anything from me, and I didn't hide anything from her. Oh my God! I was blown away. I was cool with it because they were having a great time. Besides, it was none of my business. They both were grown. Who was I to judge anyone? I was dating and in love with a married man. I had been through this several times before. I believed everything that I was told at the time. Rich was believable, and I trusted him. I was in love. It did not matter what anyone said because I was team Rich and that was it and Reed knew that we were history.

I had absolutely no room to judge anyone. Rich was not ashamed of me, nor did he care who saw us together. I loved this about him, we fucked a lot, and we spent a lot of time together on and off the ship. Every port we hit was him and I. And of course, Blackman was right there with her ship dude.

The Symptoms Started

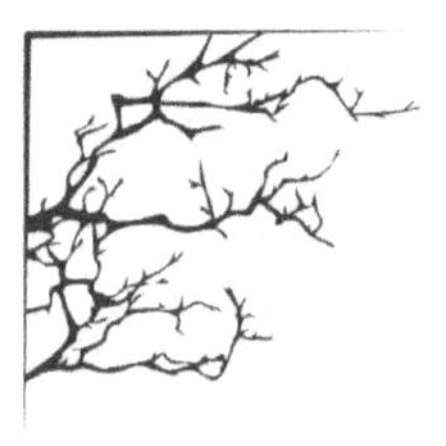

We were now getting ready for summer surge which is a cruise for four to six months. We are out to sea doing mostly nothing other than maintaining the ship. I worked in the galley which is like an extra-large kitchen. I stood on my feet a lot. I did not think anything of it when my feet began to swell. They got bigger and bigger. I decided to get it checked by the doctor and he placed me on bed rest for one day. I returned to work, and it happened again and again. But it got worse. It then moved to my eyes. My eyes became blurry daily, and I knew I was sick. Something was wrong with me. I knew this was not normal. The doctors kept sending me to my rack/bed.

The first time I believed the medical team did not believe me, but they still gave me light duty. The next time was different. Something was going on with my eyes. I was taken a lot more seriously. This time when I was checked and the doctor from Medical was able to see that my eyes were worse and saw redness. My eyes were burning, they were sensitive to light, blurry in vision, and I had floating spots. It started in the right eye and after a day or so it moved to the left eye. I was told it was inflammation of the eyes. I was almost blind, and the doctors were scared at this point. No one knew what to do. I made them nervous because my eyes burned every time the lights came on. I was always kept in the dark until the doctors had time to figure out what to do. I wore shades everywhere I went. One of the nurses gave them to me because I needed to cover my eyes due to eye sensitivity. These shades were specifically for blocking the sun and they worked perfectly. I was so scared I thought I was going blind for real. I really could not see shit! Everything was blurry. Thank God I was not completely blind. I could see a little. I needed some relief, and I needed it fast.

The medical officers did not believe me when I told them, they could have done something about this a long time ago. They thought I was faking just like everyone on the ship that came there. I didn't know what to do but at some point, the medical staff knew that they had to do something. The doctor had me pack some of my things and flew me to the USS Enterprise which was a huge aircraft carrier ship. This ship held a maximum of 4,600 military personnel and civilians. This ship held civilians, large planes, army vehicles, and some army crew members, this ship was huge.

I knew I had to leave. I needed to see Rich before I left. I had to sex him down with my blurry vision and all. I knew he was concerned about me and hated to see me go. Rich was stubborn. He did not walk with me to depart because he did not want to see me fly off. The doctors who treated me were scared and wanted me off the ship soon as possible. Hell, I was scared and concerned at how they were acting about getting me off the freaking ship. I had no answers to what was wrong with me. I had to give my best friend love before I left her alone on this crooked ship.

The medical team and someone from the officer team escorted me to the chopper. I was horrified. I was afraid of heights, small aircrafts, and my health. This had to be serious if they were flying me off the ship. You and I both wonder how in the hell I could be on a ship and afraid of heights. Honestly, I did not know how I did what I did but I knew I had to do it. But a helicopter was something else. It was loud and shaky. I had to take many deep breaths for this ride. It seemed that the freaking helicopter was going to fall out of the sky. Maybe because we were near the water, and it seemed windier. We were an oiler ship. The Enterprise was nearby.

The Aircraft carrier was huge, and it was foreign to me. I had no clue where I was, and I was terrified of course. The medical team ran out to get me and this scared me more. You would have thought I had Ebola or something. I was escorted to their medical unit and there was a bed waiting for me. This ship was nothing like the other shit it was three times bigger, and it had so many people there. I heard them all and of course, I could still see shadows when they passed by. They ran so many tests on me. YES! There was an actual eye clinic on this ship. I felt like a lab rat after all those freaking tests. The doctors checked my eye pressure, dilated my eyes, and looked at the back of my eyes. I had never heard of any of the things that they were doing to me. But I knew it had to be done to fix me.

I had a nurse to do everything for me the entire time. The female nurse had to bathe me, feed me, and dress me. I was able to email Rich. I had this cool-ass chick named Ashworth as my nurse. She was white but cool as fuck. She helped me email Rich, but when I checked my email, he had already emailed me. I smiled because I knew he missed me. After a few days of meds called prednisone; I started regaining some of my vision back. Please don't worry I was never in any pain or anything. My eyes burned and I was uncomfortable. I was able to see a little better, but I was still sensitive to light. I was now able to do things for myself. Ashworth would not leave my side.

I emailed Rich every single chance I got, and this gave me hope for us. I did not want to leave him on the ship with the vultures who wanted him. Ashworth helped me email Rich because of course I could not see too well. We continued to show our feelings to one another daily. Eventually, we said, "I love you." YES! We both did it and started saying it all the time. I knew he loved me months before we pulled back in from deployment. He knew I loved him too.

I was glad The Enterprise was able to help me out. I was better. It seemed as if something bad was wrong with me. I was never told what was wrong with me. Although they had much more equipment; they still were not able to treat me. I received new orders within days to get to the National Naval Medical Center in Bethesda Maryland. I did not know what to do or say but I knew that Reed was there, and I did not want to go. Guess what? It was not up to me to go or not go. I had to take my ass wherever they told me to go.

We were on the coast of London, which is considered The United Kingdom. (UK) To be honest I didn't know where the fuck I was. The country was amazing from what I could see. The buildings, the landscaping, the cars, how they were driving, it was nice. I thought to myself that this would be a great time to have my full eyesight. I could not get the full view of this beautiful country. I will come back one day, but without the shades. It was now time for me to leave.

I was put on a small boat to reach land. I still could not see much. Everything was still a little blurry. I had my shades, bookbag and a cane to help me walk. I looked as if I was completely blind. I needed everything they left me with. Once I reached land, I was placed in a taxi alone and I was to go to the airport. Once I arrived at the airport, I was able to get an escort assigned to me using my ID. I shopped a little inside with my escort assisting me through the airport. I bought some coffee for my mom because I do not drink it. I bought myself some tea and a few other things that caught my eye. I sat by the terminal door for me to board my flight and of course, they boarded me first and sat me right up front. I slept most of the flight, but it seemed that it took me forever to get where we were going. I was restless and uncomfortable. The flight was about eight hours or more.

Oh my, I was lost. This was not planned well. I caught a cab from JFK airport to Bethesda Md. Guess what???!!! No one was there. The place was empty. I asked a stranger question about the hospital and its hours, but she had no clue. I would have slept in the hospital lobby, but I knew I could not do that. It was the 4th of July weekend. I swallowed my pride and called the only person I knew there and that was Reed. I called and he was in New York with his girlfriend and son. Sam was his son by Phillip. I asked for suggestions, and he called around to find out where I was supposed to be. He told me to go to the hotel on the base and they would house me for however long I needed it. I thanked him for his help. He told me he would be back Tuesday, and I said OK thanks for your help.

Reed called and checked on me to make sure they handled everything correctly. I was able to get a refund for everything I paid for the entire time I was there. He was resourceful when it came to the system of the military. He was shocked that I called him, but he was glad that I called. I went to the PX to get clothes and toiletries. I also bought stuff I didn't need. This was the first time I was completely alone and had no one to talk to. I just ordered food and stayed in my room. I had no other choice but to be patient. I had to wait until the holidays were over to be seen by the doctors.

I know you guys are wondering about what happened to Reed's son, Sam. The son he supposedly had by Phillip. Well, the husband supposedly went and had a DNA test and found out that the baby was not his. He allegedly divorced her due to this. That means Reed had to take a DNA to find out if the child was his and of course, it was Reed's child 99.99999999999%. The baby mamma had to go out to sea for six months and someone had to watch him. Who else to watch their child is the actual parent? Oh, he was forced because he had no other choice. But that was his business and his problem. I was just ready to see Rich and they were due to pull in soon and I was ready.

CHAPTER 12

The Diagnosis

I went to the doctor on Tuesday morning. I saw a few specialists and received my diagnosis. I had Uveitis and Sarcoidosis. Uveitis targets the eyes; Sarcoidosis is a disease that attacks certain organs. It's inflammation of organs or cells of your body which are in your lungs and lymph nodes. But it can also affect the skin, eyes, skin, and any other organs. There is no cure for sarcoidosis but modest treatment.

I was relieved and upset at the same time. If I would have waited any longer, I could have gone blind. I now have a chronic lung disease and it was found by X-ray. I called Mom and she cried instantly. She told me to be careful and get whatever I need to get. She was so fucking pissed and wanted to sue the military and everyone else for putting me on a plane alone. She was not happy with the way the Medical Team handled my health from the beginning. They ignored my health concern. I calmly said to mom, *we cannot sue the military.*

An older white veteran talked to my mother and told her what I should do to set my life forever. She talked to a few officers at the National Naval Medical Center to ask a lot of questions. She did not understand the answers. She was still mad. She cussed and fussed at doctors, nurses, maintenance, just everyone. I told her the real people at fault were on the ship. I kept telling them I was not well. I told Mom that I would be ok. She was in North Carolina trying to help but this was something I had to figure out myself. And this is when I started my research.

Yes, I was scared! I did not know what to do. I was only 24 years old. I had a little pity party and asked God *"why me" I was too young for this sickness to take over my body. I don't want to die.* I was terrified that I could die or something. The doctor and nurses comforted me and assured me that I would be fine. They said it is a lifelong disease. Well, I knew I couldn't get myself out of this one. I had to learn to accept it. I took all kinds of medication. I had to put eye drops in my eyes every day until it cleared up. I still took birth control regularly every day. My life had suddenly changed right before my eyes. I moved to Bethesda Maryland to finish my treatment. So, I called my apartment manager to discuss my situation. I needed to get my apartment packed.

I was disappointed because I could not be with Rich. I looked forward to seeing him soon. But there was nothing that I could do other than drive back and forth to see him. I think Reed helped me get my house packed out and my car back to Maryland. I am not 100% sure, but I am almost positive it was him. After weeks in the hotel, Reed extended a deal for me to stay with him in the extra room. He proposed that I babysit his son Sam for free.

This trade-off sounded great to me. I babysat Sam while he worked. I didn't work much because I was still in treatment. Don't worry nothing happened between Reed and me. I was loyal to Rich. Reed brought several women home to fuck. He wanted to get me jealous, but it did not bother me. The only thing it did was get me ready for my man.

It was time. The ship pulled in and I was anxious to see Rich. I drove four hours to find my man. I also was excited to see Blackman as well. She was so happy to see me, and she had different friends. We chatted like we never missed a beat. She went to New York, and I went with Rich. When Rich laid eyes on me you could tell he missed me. His face lit up like a Christmas tree. He was all over me and did not care who saw us. He hugged and kissed me as if he had waited for years. I was happy and he was happy. Rich and I stayed at the hourly hotel that was nearby. Rich and I fucked all day and all night and did not leave the room not even to eat. He could not keep his hands off me. We fucked and sucked on one another all day every day. There was always porn on in the room, so we were aroused more and more for one another.

I interrupted Rich in the heat of the moment to tell him that I was on a lot of drugs and my birth control may not work effectively. He said, "I don't care." I'm thinking to myself like *Ok, Let's keep fucking, but I do not want any babies. I have other things I must deal with. I don't even have my other son with me now. Why would I be trying to have a baby?* I did my part by telling him about the possible side effects of my medicine. I kept taking my birth control. Eventually, we had to separate. I had to get back to the hospital and he had to go home to his wife. I drove back home feeling good and fulfilled with the love I just received from my man. I continued my treatment, and the doctors eventually sent me to CDC (Central

Distribution Center) inside the hospital to work in a distribution department in the basement. It's where they distribute all medical supplies. I worked the desk. I was on light duty until the Sarcoidosis cleared up or became more stable.

I started to feel sick and nauseated. It had been at least six weeks since Rich and I had sex. I immediately knew that I was pregnant. It was probably about eight weeks when I got tested and officially found out I was pregnant. Rich and I talked every day, and we were still on good terms, and he knew that Reed and I were not together. We were basically roommates. I babysat his son in exchange for a room in his apartment. Blackman was the first person I broke the news to that I was pregnant. I told her that I could not have a baby right now.

Rich was married and with his wife. I also did not want to kill a baby either. So many thoughts ran through my mind: *I had just started my career in the military, and I wanted to save much more money. I did not want to be struggling with another kid. I already do not have my son. I wanted a house and a nice car. I knew that another child would slow that down, and this is Rich's baby and he's married.* I already knew that was going to be a problem. Whenever a baby comes up you see people/niggas true colors. Blackman gave me some good advice. She told me to tell Rich before I got too far along. I didn't tell Reed away.

I called Rich and told him I needed to talk to him, and it was extremely important. He asked if he could call me back because he was busy. He seemed to be happy to hear my voice when he called. I said to him, Rich *you remember I told you that my birth control probably will not work due to the medication they had me on,* he remembered. He then said, "Are you saying that you are pregnant?"

I said *Yes, I am 10 weeks*. He seemed so concerned and asked what I wanted to do. I told him that I was not ready to have a baby and I did not want to kill one either. I asked him if he could help me with the baby if I had it.

A few days passed and Rich suggested that I have an abortion and I went with it. It sounded like Rich was not ready for that step with me. I was a little sad and confused because I thought he loved me. I thought he wanted to be with me. He sent me the money quickly to get this procedure done as soon as possible. I put my big girl panties on and went to get this done. I was ready. I had no choice. I was scared to death.

Blackman and Reed went with me to get the abortion. I was still confused, hurt, and sad. It was an unexplainable hurt that took a toll on me. That shit was serious and scary. I did not want to have an abortion, but I thought it was for the best. I did not want to disappoint Rich. I sat there waiting with the palms of my hands sweating, legs shaking, heart beating extra fast, mouth dry, and my brain thinking a million things at once. The nurse called me to the back to get bloodwork done. I patiently waited for my turn. My name was called. I laid on the table in my paper gown and my blanket. I was ready. I had my feet in the serapes and legs wide open. The doctor walked back into the room and said to me, "we cannot do an abortion on you. Your white blood count is extremely low, the calcium in your blood is high, and your ACE (angiotensin-converting enzyme) range is high. If you have this procedure you could bleed to death. The doctor stated that I would most likely die if I got an abortion. "You have to get your O2 (oxygen saturation.) Sat's together and your blood counts together." The doctor referred me to go back to the hospital. That's how out of control my health was.

I was nervous, confused, and scared. I asked the doctor how long it would take for me to get my Oxygen Saturation under control. Will I have time to have a healthy baby? I guess it was one of those unpredictable situations. I hoped I could carry the baby to full term. The doctor was sure about this: "We do not recommend you have an abortion because you could die." I was pissed and happy. I did not want to die. I did not want to have an abortion. I have so much more to do with my life. This was a sign from God telling me to have this baby. I have plans for you guys. Mom was totally against abortions. I told her about this, and she cussed me out for almost two months.

I called Rich to tell him the news. I told him that I would send him his money back. He told me to keep it for diapers. He didn't say much but he sounded disappointed. Rich didn't ask me about my health or the baby. I brushed it off because I felt that he needed to process this. This was a big life change for us both. Rich behavior changed in the upcoming weeks. He started acting differently and our conversations were shorter. My excitement for us was short-lived. I thought he would help me throughout my pregnancy and with our baby. Time passed and he acted as if he did not care anymore. His loving and caring behavior had changed. You already know what was next. Yes, he questioned if the baby was his. I was shocked that he would even ask that. I guess someone told his wife something because he kept saying shit like "are you sure the baby is mine and not Reed's?" *No nigga you and I know who baby this is. I am not fucking Reed.* I was so disappointed, and I felt really stupid.

Oh, Fuck!!! Here I am alone and pregnant. I bet Reed was thinking, "That's what you get" Yep, I fucked up and I just had to suck it up and get over it. Four months had passed, and our conversations stopped altogether. He did not want to have anything else to do with me. He ghosted me completely. One day I texted Rich, *I know we are not talking or whatever but all I ask is that you just give me $400 a month for child support.* He texted me and said "the baby is not mine, so I am not helping you with shit. I never even loved or cared for you" Tears fell down my face because I thought that he was different from every other guy I ever dealt with. I was depressed and did not know what to do. I was so sad. I thought about how stupid I had been. *I deserved this shit, for what I had done and was doing.* I was fucking around with a married man. I dumped Reed for Rich. I had a reality check. I knew he would never leave his wife. One of the excuses he told me was "if I leave, she's going to take everything from me." How could I be so young and stupid?

I sat at Reed's house and felt sorry for myself. It was time for me to move on and get my health together. I took care of my health and rested as much as possible as the doctor suggested. My job made sure that I was always seated. I needed to block it all out and move on with my life. I was about six months pregnant, and I eventually had sex with Reed. We had sex about three times. It was mostly him giving me oral just so I could Nutt. It did not mean anything to me. I needed sex to keep my sanity. Stress kicked in and it seemed my Sarcoidosis had gotten worse. My body had begun to shift negatively.

I worked at the National Naval Medical Center to make sure I received proper treatment for my Sarcoidosis and my pregnancy. On my way from work, I stopped at a small booth in the hospital and ordered bean soup. I felt weird. I did not feel well. I wanted to make it home and get in my bed. I knew something was wrong. I ate the bean soup in the middle of the hospital. I had never had it before, and it was delicious. I looked outside and it was snowing hard. After I ate the soup, I walked to my car to drive to Reed's house. I was twenty-eight weeks into my pregnancy. I thought to myself, *I cannot have this baby right now.* There was snow everywhere and I was scared to drive. I made it to my car, and I could hear my mother's voice saying, "take your ass back into that hospital and have them check you because it's their job."

I walked back into the hospital on the baby floor and told a nurse that I did not feel good. The nurse walked me to the back, and she checked my little guy's heartbeat. I peed in the cup. The nurse said the baby's heartbeat was fine and it was routine to collect pee when you are pregnant. The nurse said my little guy's heartbeat was good. I was sent home. I hopped on the elevator. I was happy that I was able to go home and that nothing was wrong. I headed to my car and looked up and saw a nurse running toward me. She grabbed my hand and said, "baby you have to come back upstairs." so, now I am worried. I asked her *Is my baby ok?"* she looked at me and said "Yes, but you have a lot of protein in your urine." Protein in your urine while pregnant means that there is something wrong. I had pre-eclampsia and or extremely high blood pressure which was not good at all. I walked back in, and the nurse gave me some medicine to help my baby become stronger. The nurse gave me a shot and then Reed walked in. Yes! I said Reed because I had no one else to call.

My mother was eight or more hours away. You best believe Mary B would have been on her way. She would have her feet on the pedal going full speed. I was put in a room and told to chill out. Everyone was running around as if something was wrong. No one told me what was wrong. The nurse gave me another shot. Reed and I sat there chatting and laughing. My little man was kicking the shit out of my tummy. Suddenly, I felt horrible, and I felt my eyes roll to the back of my head and I could feel myself shaking. I heard Reed scream as he ran out of the room, to get help. I blacked out after that.

I woke up two days later and I looked around like, this *is it? Am I dead?* Everything was white and blurry. I opened my eyes and I saw my mom yelling. I heard her say "She's up! Thank you, Jesus! she woke up." The nurse came in to check on me. She said, "how do you feel?" I nodded my head yes because I had a tube in my mouth. The nurses took everything off me. I asked the nurse, *where is my baby?*" she looked at me and said "He's a fighter just like you. He's in the NICU. He weighs 1 lb. 15 oz. Do you want to pump him some milk?" The nurse said breast milk would be better to help him gain weight. I pumped milk right away and I was so glad he was ok.

A few days later I was able to see my baby. I walked into the NICU and guess who was there? Reed and my mom! I smiled. Oh My! My baby boy was the size of my hand. He opened one eye when he felt my presence. I cried. It seemed as if he was in pain. I still wanted him to have something of his father, so I named him Charcell Jahem Hargrove aka CJ. He was born on January 20, 2005, at 11:28 pm. I saw him every single day. I did not miss a day. A month later the doctor asked me to sign a paper to resuscitate him if he passed away. I said, *if he goes, let him go.* The doctor said to me "we are giving him two weeks to live. If he has the open-heart surgery everything goes well, he could live." All I could think about is the poor baby that was next to him. He had the same surgery and he died. I told the doctor *No, I cannot let you guys cut into my son's chest, I can't do that.*

I did not let them do the heart surgery that they originally wanted to do but I did let them do a procedure in which they needed to put an IV catheter in his head. They shaved one side of his head to place the IV on the right side of his head. That was the only way to give him the fluids and medication he needed. The feeding tube was attached to his nose. He had to have a tracheotomy. This was a surgical procedure in which an incision (hole) in his neck(throat). This gave him the oxygen he needed to survive. He could not breathe on his own. It was so hard for me to watch my "CJ" like this. I cried every time I saw him. If this did not make me strong, I didn't know what else in my life would. I needed to be strong, but everyone around me knew that I was hurting behind my beautiful smile. It was written all over my face. I pumped milk every chance I got. I wanted what was best for him, but I did not want him to suffer.

The doctor was honest with me and told me to not get my hopes up. He said CJ may not make it. Another told me that my baby had two weeks to live. He asked me if I wanted to resuscitate him again. I told the doctor, no if it's his time then it will be his time. I said to the doctor, *He looks at me every day and he will be just fine. He knows what's in store for him here with me. CJ will be just fine,* I had faith. I waited for my son to get better. He was changing my life. I valued life so much more now. CJ and Donny were my reason for living and they inspired me to try and make better decisions for us. This was by far the hardest thing I had to deal with in my life. You will never know love until you have a child.

CJ was four months old when he was moved to the Children's Hospital in Washington DC. The whole team of military doctors expressed to me that I needed to get a residence to live in. So, when CJ became strong enough to come home, he would have somewhere stable to go. As well the 24-hour nurses will have a room. The military will pay for all the accommodations.

I guess one of the doctors contacted someone high in the chain of command and expressed concern about keeping the father's name private. Because I received a call from a JAG (Judge Advocate General) officer. The doctor told her that I needed more help and support. The Judge Advocate General (JAG) is an Advisor of the Navy for all legal matters dealing with the Navy. Navy. She asked me if I had any help with raising CJ. I told her *No*, but I had tried to get his father to help. I asked him for $400 a month and I would not contact the child support office. All I needed was a little help. She said, "let's call him." She handed me the phone and said "here you try to do this again your way. Then we can do this my way if he doesn't want to cooperate. Maybe we can see where his head is and figure out how to get you some help. I expressed to her that I did not want to get him in trouble.

This was just as much my fault as well. I agreed after she talked to me for about an hour. I was stressed and exhausted. I could not do this alone and I hated that I put myself in this situation. The more she talked to me the more I came to my senses. I did not make CJ myself and we needed help. Why am I saving him? Especially knowing that he said CJ wasn't his and how he did not want to have anything to do with us. *Why was I still trying to save him?* Why did I still love this inconsiderate, ungrateful, heartless motherfucker?

I honestly did not want anyone to get in trouble and I made sure I drilled that into the JAG officer. She assured me that she understood. She looked at me and said "Let's just see if he will take responsibility and man up and we wouldn't have to report anything. I'm here to help you." We called Rich and he answered. I told him that the officer was there with me. I told him all I needed was a little help and no one else had to get involved. He said, "that is not my baby, and you need to call Reed." The officer wrote down and recorded everything he and his wife said.

I said to him that we can get a blood test. He continued saying "I know that baby is not mine because Reed told me you and he had been fucking since you got to Maryland." Lies!!! I clearly and calmly said *I do not want anyone to get in trouble. I just need a little help. CJ is on life support, and I am going to need help, he will need 24-hour care.* Brenda, his wife, got on the phone and went off cursing "do what the fuck you gotta do because that's not his baby" The JAG officer asked for the phone. She tried to talk to Brenda. She told her "She is not trying to get anyone in any trouble. She just wants help with their child." Brenda told the officer, "Do what you have to do, but I know for a fact that it is not his baby." Well, that pissed the JAG officer off!! She was so mad she turned whiter than she already was. She said to me, "it is out of your hands now. I am going to handle it from here."

I did not hear anything from her for about two weeks or so. CJ was still in the NICU in DC. I got a call from the JAG Officer asking me to meet her at the Children's Hospital to give CJ a paternity test. I had to sign papers and I had to get my mouth swabbed as well. Rich was in Jacksonville, Florida, and was swabbed there. *And lord behold he is the father 99.99999999999999%.* Hell, I already knew that he was the father. I know who I fucked and did not fuck. I mean, I tried to defuse the situation by just asking for help. I did not plan for it to go this far. But Rich and his wife wanted to handle the situation another way. Even with all the nasty words and lies, I still did not want Rich to get in trouble. I loved Rich and I thought he loved me. It took a lot for me to talk to the JAG officer about the situation.

I had a kind heart. I was not thinking of myself or how I was going to take care of my disabled child. I was more concerned about saving Rich. One day Mom said to me, "Fee you can't save everyone, and you can't let everyone get over on you. You tried to do the right thing and he decided to do the wrong thing." She was right. I knew his wife hated me and was upset about what happened as she should be. But all the blame was not on me. All of this could have been avoided with one simple agreement. They were trying to prove a point, but it backfired. They fucked their own family Rich was Court Martialed. Court Martial is worse than Captain's Mast. It is a judicial court for military personnel accused of wrongdoing against the military law. Rich was charged with an inappropriate relationship with someone under him, which was me. He could get jail time, dishonorable discharge, or be forced to retire.

I was finally able to get an apartment that accommodated CJ and his equipment. I was now able to move Donny in with us. We were now a family. I was so ready for family life. I enrolled Donny in school. I loved going school shopping for him and I loved putting him on the bus. I was exhausted and happy as hell. I had both my boys with me, and they loved their mother. We lived in the same apartment complex right around the corner from Reed and his ex-wife's apartment. What a coincidence.

There was some good news. CJ was better. I was able to take him home at six months. He was still small but much bigger to hold on to. He was chunky and full of life. He smiled a lot. It was hard to notice his condition. You only knew it because he had a trach. We all learned sign language because CJ could not talk. We needed to communicate to know when he was hungry and to get his needs met.

Reed did play a good role in CJ's life for a little while until he went back to his ways. Now that CJ was better, I knew it was a matter of time before the courts would call for us to go to Court Martial.

The JAG office and the Military team sent me CJ plane tickets to Jacksonville, Florida for Court Martial. We were put in a hotel for the days we were there. They made sure that CJ had all the necessary things for the plane ride. CJ had to be always on oxygen. I thought this court stuff was for child support, but when we got there, I saw that it was more to it than I thought. They expected me to have my uniform on as I was on trial as well. I blamed Brenda for all this shit because we could have handled this with just $400 a month. *I do not want your husband anymore Brenda.* I've had all of him already and I also have a child with him. I do not want him anymore after the way he handled this situation.

I went on the stand and told them that I was only there to get help for my child. I did not want anyone to lose their positions in the military. I wasn't concerned about him and his wife's relationship. I explained to the courts about CJ's condition and the severity of it. I almost died giving birth and I am happy that we both are here now. It was time for Rich and his wife to get the fuck over it. He is my miracle child, and I do not regret him at all. God wanted him here with me and I will cherish every moment. I told him that he was the one missing out on this wonderful child. It is your loss and not mine. He testified and said he was wrong, and he should not have done so. He went into a spill about his mother dying while he was in the military, and he shed a few tears. I had heard that story before from Reed. He told the same story when he went to Captain's Mast. I am sorry that they both lost their mothers while serving our country, but they still had to take responsibility for their actions.

After the court trial I packed up our bags and we went straight to the Airport. They released me before the case was over. I did not know what the verdict was. I was just ready to get home. I later found out that they forced him to retire. We were at our gate early. I heard my name over the intercom stating that there was a call for me, and I needed to pick up the closest phone. They gave me a number to dial. I did just that thinking it was the JAG officer. To my surprise it was Rich. He asked why I left so fast. I was surprised and speechless. I told him that I didn't think he wanted to have anything to do with us. He wanted to see his son. He was nice and talked as if nothing had happened. I believe we saw him and his wife at the airport before we left. I was unsure because CJ and I were headed home on our flight. That was the last day I heard from Rich.

CHAPTER 13

In Between it All

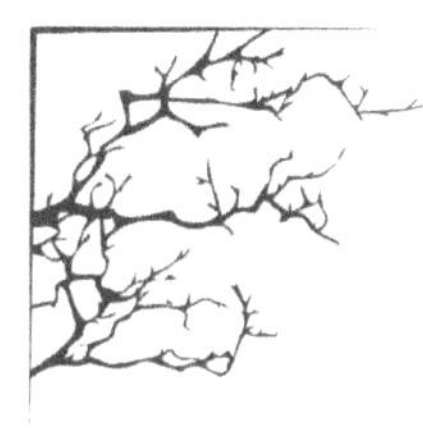

I needed sex. It had been a tough six months having CJ in the NICU. I was in need and Reed was doing his own thing and wasn't thinking about me. I understood and he wasn't the only nigga on the planet. However, I did not approach men. They had to come for me. I was single and that was clear between Reed and me. I met Greg at the hospital where I worked. Greg was about 6ft 5in tall, real solid, about 350 pounds, and he had a nice smile. I did not pay him any mind, but he kept fucking with me. Every time I left for lunch to pump milk; he was somewhere flirting. The flirting went on for a few weeks. He finally invited me for drinks. I took him up on his offer and went out with him. But everyone that worked in the office was also there. We kissed in the car. Oh Wow! He could kiss. Yes! In my mind, if you can kiss you can eat pussy. If you could not kiss, then I would walk off. No second chances with that, because that was a fucking turn-off. Well, Greg did well in that department.

We started hanging out a lot. We met at the club for drinks. I felt that this was a bad idea, but I was needy. I did not know why I attracted hoes. Greg was a hoe, but he was great at hiding it. He made you feel good about yourself and spiked your head up. There was one major problem with Greg, he lied about being married. Oh wait, there is more. He was also in another relationship with some girl that worked in the same area we worked in. I found out all of this AFTER I fucked him.

The sex was always a quick fuck. We had sex at the hotel a few times but not many. We fucked a lot in the car, bathroom, or wherever. He had a huge dick. Oh, my goodness! But after a while, I did not want to have sex with him. We used condoms all the time. One day the condom burst. OH SHIT! I was scared. Birth control was not effective for me because it seemed that my body rejected it. Either I bled for months, or I ended up pregnant. I became pregnant with both Donny and CJ on birth control. So, when the condom burst, I was terrified. I knew I was fertile as hell. I cannot be pregnant! CJ was only six months old and on life support. I looked up to the ceiling begging God to help me. Lord knows I could not handle another child. I guess I was getting punished again. I just couldn't catch a break from the bullshit.

Of course, I was fucking sick and had all the "you are pregnant bitch" symptoms. I was definitely pregnant, and it was strong. Strong like that shit would show up in seconds of pissing on the stick. I said to myself, *I cannot go through this shit again. I just can't deal with nearly dying trying to have a baby and I cannot be raising any more children on my own.*

I had just found out that Donny's father who has NEVER done anything for him had gone to jail and they gave him 30 years. I now have two children with both their fathers not in the picture. Rich was only paying child support and Donny's daddy Trey was locked up. These sperm donors are getting more and more trashy. The answer was fucking NO for me. I told Greg that I was pregnant and that we had to get rid of it now. I told him I could not handle raising any more children alone. He claimed that I would not be alone. NOPE!! *Fool me once shame on you, fool me twice shame on me, fool me three times I am a big fucking dummy.* NO SIR!!! He found the place and paid for it. I went the next day and got checked and the doctor said it was two. Oh, hell no!! I did not want to see any more ultrasounds. I thought to myself; I was going to pretend that was a glimpse because it made me feel worse knowing that it was two. I could not take care of any more babies. I was not going to put myself in the position to be homeless, broke, or back in North Carolina. HELL NO!!

Please do not judge me!!! But I was not ready for more babies! I hate that I put myself in this situation again. I went to the clinic the next day to have the procedure done. The procedure was done in Maryland. It was the hardest thing I had to do in my life. If I had been stable or hit the lottery, I would not have had an abortion. I would love them all the same. This was bad timing and CJ was still on life support and had two nurses at home with him. How would I look walking around pregnant again? I needed to get my health together. I was still having symptoms of sarcoidosis. My blood count was still rocky. I was sad but it had to be done. I had to put my big girl panties on and get shit done.

I did not fuck with Greg again. He begged and begged, and he still begs until this day. I kept my pussy to myself for a while. I feared dick at this time. I still worked with the girls Greg was fucking. He begged for my panties because he wanted to smell them. I gave them to him because I knew I was not giving him any more of my goodies. I was not going to risk it and besides, his dick was too big. I didn't know how I took all of that. I loved my walls but clearly, his dick was a wall burster. I had to soak every time I fucked him.

Having sex with Greg was not a comfortable fuck. I could not enjoy the penetration. If the dick is over nine inches and the size of a fist, I do not want it. *Lesson learned.* I will start asking men for their dick size from here on out. I am curious to know why women like men with huge dicks. What does it do for them? To each her own, I guess. From my experience, I noticed that men with big dicks can't eat pussy. Most of them anyway. The ones that can are not selfish. That is a plus because most men with big dicks feel privileged and think that is enough. Oh, no foreplay is what gets me ready for the dick. You can't just be sticking stuff in me and have not tasted it yet.

He was a good guy, but he was also a male hoe. He had girls everywhere. The good thing about him being a hoe was that he moved on quickly. He did not get attached and he just fuck'em and kept moving to the next one. That was the first time I was so happy about that shit. I'm glad I did not get attached to him as I did with the other ones I had dealt with. I dodged a bullet.

CHAPTER 14

Life Goes On

Life goes on and I had to keep my head held high. Everything was going well. I still lived in my apartment and Donny was in school. CJ was growing stronger by the day. We lived comfortably. I went to work and drove back home when I could. Reed and I talked from time to time. We hung out and had drinks a few times together. Whenever my family came down, he let us in the club for free. Reed helped me as a friend would. But he hit a roadblock and needed my help at this time. Allegedly his ex-wife called the housing people, or the housing people called her, and he was reported. Reed was not supposed to be in the apartment at all. He had to move out and pay back $28,000-$30,000 or more. I allowed him to move in with me for a little while until he saved up or whatever. It was my turn to return the favor.

I began thinking deeply about life and I wanted more for my family. I decided to enroll in a bartending school in Arlington,

Virginia. I drove there every day. It was about 45 minutes away from home. My nurses were helpful. They watched Donny after school while I was in class. It did not take long for me to get my license. I felt more accomplished and empowered because I was taking charge of my life. I met new people and learned more things about myself. I started bartending at Andrews Airforce Base and made extra money. I saved for us again. Everything seemed to be going good until...

One night, I left work from the bar and a scary incident happened. I had only two drinks, but something was wrong. I felt weird as I drove home. I started feeling worse and worse. I blanked out, but I remembered a little. I was not good with directions. However, I know that I took the same route home every day. I had no clue where I was or who I was. I just knew something was wrong with me. I drove on the wrong side of the road. By the Grace of God, I made it to the store and some lady helped me. She explained to Reed where I was. I had already dialed the number I just didn't know where I was. Someone spiked my drink with something. Reed came and they gave me water. The lady told Reed that it seemed that someone put something in my drink because of how I was acting, and I was sweating. I remember very little about that night. I do know that I should have been in jail for a DWI or dead. I dodged a huge bullet. Reed was pissed and I was embarrassed for allowing this shit to happen to me. I was good at watching my drink intake. I was convinced someone put something in my drink because I knew better.

I made good money at Andrews Airforce Base bar and grill. There were a lot of old retired guys there and they came there just to sit at the bar. They left nice tips. Some were just living on the base and had nothing else to do. I enjoyed working there but after that incident, I decided to quit. I felt that someone was out to get me.

I did not feel safe. Guess what? One night I met Mel there, he was passing through. I think I gave him false hopes because he thought we were going to fuck, hang out, or be together or something. I had been treated like shit and Reed kept saying that we were not together.

During the holiday Reed and I got back together. I don't know how it happened. Maybe he felt sorry for me or maybe he wanted to be with me. We made it official around January of 2006. So, we started our new journey together and I was ready. We fucked on the regular and had so much fun going to sex parties all kinds of shit. We were having fun!! We were having fun like we used to. Well, I guess I had too much fun with his ass because I had a feeling he was cheating again. Man...you would think that he learned his lesson the last time. HELL NO! He did not. He did not last a year without cheating. I requested to get out of CDC and move to the Galley where I belong. Cooking.

I had been a good girl, and it took a lot for me to not get even. I knew he worked at the club and his weakness was women. I guess he could not handle all the attention from women. He lost control. He thought he could outsmart me, but he always got caught. I placed a tape recorder in his car for a few days. I did this when he was on his way to work at the club. I had to find the right time because I missed the action. I guess I put it there too early. Then one day it was perfect, but his truck was so loud shifting gears and shit I could only hear the floor rattling. So, I put it on something soft. A place I knew it would not rattle and a place I knew he would not find it. I later listened to the recording. I CAUGHT HIM!

He was talking to some girl discussing how he played in the girl's pussy and the girl was foreign. He repeated everything she said. He acted like he was a teenager. The girl said to him "you were playing in my pussy" and Reed repeated it and said, "I did play in that pussy." I confronted him a few days later and I let him listen to the recording. He lied and blew it off. I asked him several times if he was cheating and who was that girl. He lied. He said he didn't know her, and it was not him.

I played inspector gadget and did some investigating of my own. I believe I pretended to be him on the phone for them to send the bill to me. The phone records showed actual texts on this bill. That was a no-no and they sent it to me. Again, he cheated and talked to a bunch of foreign girls. Most of them did not speak English well. This girl I called spoke English until I told her I was Reed's girlfriend. Then she started speaking in whatever language the bitch spoke.

One day I drove from Hyattsville, Maryland to Washington, DC to catch Reed. I drove to his job and watched him at the door. He was doing the normal flirting, smiling, touching, and having a great time at work. Then a black SUV pulled up with dark windows right beside me. I looked crazy because no one ever paid attention to me. He rolled the back window down which meant he was someone. He had a personal driver. He introduced himself as Kenith and he was tall and slim. He was dressed very well and smelled great. He had a great talk game and asked a lot of questions. He asked why I was out so late alone. I explained why I was out there. He told me he knew Reed. He said that Reed had a different girl every night at work. I was so upset. He asked for my number, and I gave it to him. He called the next day and asked me to meet him, and I did. We met at the park first and we kissed, and I told him I could not have sex with him. He became really upset and threaten to call Reed and tell him we had been having sex for a year. I was so scared.

I had to have sex with him. I went home in shame. I said I was not going to talk to him anymore. He then called and said to meet him at the park again and I said no. He recited Reed's number and threatened to call him. He hung up and called right back and said, "Are you coming?" I said *Yes* and met him again at the same park in a different area. This time he wanted to fuck outside the car, and he put two condoms on because the last time he nutted fast with one condom. He still didn't last long. I felt like trash. I learned what blackmail was at this time. He called two days later and said to meet him again. I said fuck no, he threatened to tell Reed again. I told him *no worries I will tell him my fucking myself. I was not fucking your dirty ass ever again.* I knew he was famous or had money or something. I just didn't understand why he wanted to do this to me. Why do I keep putting myself in these situations?

At some point I was like fuck it I can't keep chasing Reed and getting caught in other shit. I just can't. I told him to get his shit and get out. I told him that I did not care where he went but it will not be here. I told him that I was sending the kids to North Carolina. He straightened up quickly. One day as we were riding down the road, he tried to propose to me with no ring. I said to him how are you proposing to me with no ring? I can't take you seriously. I said you are not serious so *NO*. Two days later he came to me with a ring. I took on the challenge of becoming his wife.

I started planning for our wedding. I was excited! I've always wanted to be married and have a family. I've never been married before and he seemed so genuine. He seemed to love me, and he has always been there to help me over the years. We traveled to Georgia to visit his family. He introduced me as "his wife." I believed he was ready. I bought everything for the wedding. I bought the gowns for the ladies. I bought all the flowers online to make the arrangements. My aunt Trina helped me out as well. I placed small pictures of us on the Bahamas cruise and the coasters. It was super cheap. We traveled to North Carolina and got our marriage license on September 11, 2006. A stranger was our witness. He looked like a drunk or a crackhead.

We had our wedding ceremony on April 14, 2007. Our wedding was Beautiful. Our wedding colors were red and black. I found the best dress in North Carolina at a vintage shop for less than $200. The two old white ladies that sold it to me seemed so happy for me. The dress was beautiful, and it had a long tail. It fit me perfectly. I was living for the moment, and I was loving the moment. Our wedding was outside by the lake at Vance Granville Community College in Henderson, North Carolina. Blackman was my maid of honor and of course, my sisters were as well. Reed's nieces were at the wedding. He chose his groomsmen; my brother was included. It was much better than I thought. I could not have done it without my auntie Trina. She did a great job. The wedding cost us less than $5000 and the money was well spent. I was proud of myself for how well I got everything done alone because his ass didn't help.

The honeymoon stage did not last long and there was nothing much different about being married. One difference was me being introduced as his wife. He was good for a little while. It did not take long before Reed's attention went elsewhere especially when it came to women. One day he introduced me to a Hispanic lady named Ann. That is what he told me her name was. We partied and hung out together and we traveled on a cruise together. I became suspicious because I couldn't understand why this girl was always with us. I knew something was up when he started arguments just to leave the house. Ann stayed near us. He never admitted to fucking around with one of Ann's friends or sister. I played along like a good girl, and I wrote everything down in my journal daily.

Once we got married, he thought I was his property and that I would never leave him. That was his thought process at the time. I think this is the reason he rushed to ask me to marry him. I believe he knew I was a good woman and wife material. He did not want anyone else to have me. He wanted to basically have his cake and eat it too. He wanted me to stick around until he was ready to settle down. Why has this man not learned his lesson YET? I have no clue. But Mr. Reed NEVER LEARNED!! NEVER!! There is only so much a woman could take.

I tried to do what I needed to do to be a good wife. I was not living by my philosophy of getting revenge. But it was getting hard because it took a lot of pretending to keep him happy. I went to sex parties and allowed him to have sex with one person at the party. I was not enough and the things I allowed him to do to please him were not enough. Now I was beginning to understand what Mel meant when he said, "people are going to do what they want to do. They are not going to be ready and it's up to you to stay until they get ready. You don't have to stay but if you do you are asking for whatever you get."

I met an interesting lesbian couple. Devin and her wife Tiny seemed to be so in love. They had the house with the white picket fence and the dogs. They had several house parties that ended up with everyone fucking. Reed introduced me to them and told me what was about to happen, and I went with it. I tried to get into it but for some reason, I could not. I did not like those kinds of parties.

I went along with it though for Reed. I let a girl eat my pussy while Reed fucked her. I never had an orgasm while doing any of these things with him.

One time he introduced me to this girl named Candace and she was a healthy, thick, and mixed-race girl. She was mixed red with nice hair, but she seemed a little goofy. Reed knew what he was doing trying to fuck her. It seemed that the girl already kind of knew what was about to go down. I'm guessing we were about to have a threesome. I did not like it once again. She ate my pussy while Reed fucked her. She was soooooooooo loud as if it was hurting so bad. Reed looked at me and I looked at him and you can tell that he was losing interest because of all the screaming. It was such a turn-off. It was an experience that I did not want to have anymore.

We started hanging with Devin and Tiny a little more. We had good times, but something was not right. We never saw them two participate in any of these sex parties they had. They volunteered Reed and me to participate. I was over it, but it seemed as if Reed was not. I was beginning to think he set it all up. I started thinking of random stories he told me. One was about the time he went to another country and he and one of his buddies brought a girl to the room and he was supposed to go first. So, he started to fuck her and noticed it was a man. He then asked his friend to go first. He let his friend fuck her without telling him he was a man. I knew he was lying by the way he told the story.

A guy named Taylor from the ship told me that they thought he was gay. One day a random gay guy told me to "watch him because he's a little slick with it." I brushed it off ignored it and told whoever gossiping that my nigga cheat with too much pussy to have a gay bone in his body. I did not think anything else of it because he was my husband and that's that.

CHAPTER 15

New Orders

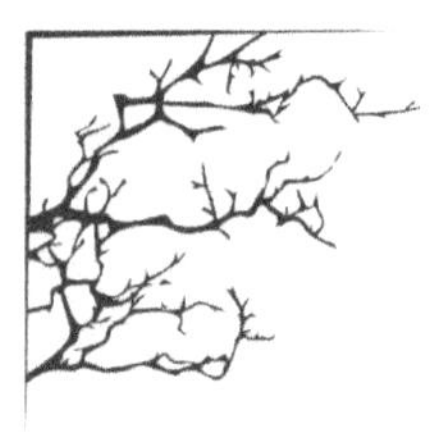

My orders were for Virginia. I was going to take the whole family to Virginia of course. The logic that Reed gave me made more sense. He said it was not good to move CJ around too much and all his doctors were in Maryland. I thought maybe he was right.

My first day on the ship was awkward and new. I was on this gigantic ship with thousands of people and this time I can see. I met new people and learned so many new things. However, I came upon a problem when I first got there. Rich and my supervisor knew each other. Master Chief Dozy and Rich kept tabs on me. Dozy gave Rich information on me the entire time. I had no clue. Rich emailed me talking about his high-ranking friend on the ship. I told Reed and he started investigating. I could tell how my new officer started treating me. Why was he still stuck on me when he was the one who did not want to have anything to do with his son? Why does he even care what I do or who talked to me?

I called Reed. I needed to get my new husband involved and that was not good for them. He went over everyone's head and informed them that my Master Chief was giving information to someone who was not on the ship. Rich was in his feelings. It seems that he wanted them to treat me like shit for the time I was there. His plan did not work. Reed made sure of that. He emailed the highest-ranking officer on the ship and explained the situation. I had a good time after the bullshit was settled. Rich didn't even give me time to settle in on my new ship. He made sure his friend knew we had a kid together but told him I trapped him.

Reed and I decided to have a baby. The plan was to get me off the ship because shit here was getting a little out of control. I did not trust my higher-ups and their connections. Rich was upset over some things that happened in the past. He and his wife were responsible. They should have accepted my $400-a-month child support deal. Everything could have been so smooth. I was not the one to blame. Life was too short to dwell on the small stuff. I loved Rich and gave him my all. Yes, I knew he was married and so did he. It was time for him to let go of the grudges because I did. I left the past in the past and he needed to as well. He did not need to try to make my life difficult.

I worked in the Galley (kitchen) for a while. We had several Galleys on the ship, and I worked on them all. I met many new people. I drove home every weekend when I was off the ship. I had no one to turn to visit for my first few months there. I could not stay away from my boys. I missed my family. I did not trust Reed with them. He was so occupied with himself that I felt that he did not deserve a family. What was I thinking? I knew Reed was a cheater. He chose to cheat rather than spend time with his family. He worked at a hospital in Washington, DC, and at a nightclub. He stayed busy when I was home. We didn't even have sex. Seriously? I had been away from home all week and we did not have sex. I then drove back to Maryland every weekend because his ass was so busy with "work".

After a while shit got lonely. He knew I was not going to do anything about it. He took me for granted. He knew I was not the type to cheat back now that we were married. *nigga you should know that you CAN NOT keep doing this to me, and think I am going to just sit here and do nothing.* I let it go on and on. He did not change no matter how much I cried or expressed my feelings. He did not want to go to counseling because he felt he was too good for that. He did not see any wrong with his actions. This was hard. I did not feel loved, and I was not getting fucked. What's a girl to do? I even started doubting myself. I knew I was not ugly, and I was not broken. I had a good head on my shoulders, and I was a good girl. What the fuck? Should I start my bald-headed hoe shit or stay a great wife? I had been a great wife and did the right thing.

Reed and I did not talk on the phone much when I was away or when I was home. It was just me and the kids. He was never home. He stayed at the club. Yes, he worked there. I felt like he cheated after he left. I followed him to the club to see if he was there and he was. But when he left, he didn't come straight home. I did not have a good sense of direction so I could not keep up with him. I needed proof that he was cheating because I was getting out soon. I did not want to carry on with an unhappy marriage. I wanted to be happy and that is what I always wanted. *Was that too much to ask for?*

I was on the ship for four months and I had learned the routine. I worked and drove home on the weekends. I rarely rested and was stressed to the max. I worked on the ship. Then I traveled back home to work. I cleaned the house, washed clothes, and made sure the boys' school things were together. The nurses were still there Thank God. I thought Reed was fucking one of the nurses or wanted to fuck one of them. I would never know. But it seriously seemed like he was fucking around with Lucy because of how he acted around her. They were alone a lot. Reed did not care who he slept with. It could have been my friend, family, co-worker, and nurse. I was exhausted! I was tired from all this investigating. I was tired of fussing and just did not care a fuck.

One day Reed found a letter that Donny's daddy Trey had written me, and he was so fucking mad. I said *the nigga is in jail and we do still have a child together*. He felt I did not need to talk to him. Yes, he said some inappropriate things, but I was not. I did not flirt back. Trust me I do not want Trey's ass. He had been in prison for years and there was nothing I could do with him. I sent him a few dollars for underwear because I felt sorry for him. But I let him know that there would never be he and I. We were NEVER in a relationship. We fucked when I was 18. I fucked him only when I wanted to. I could count on one hand how many times we had sex.

Reed was just trying to find something on me because of his fuck ups. He knew what he had been doing and he knew he was wrong. He was waiting for me to mess up. The only thing he had was me receiving a letter from my child's father from prison. He made it into something huge. *Fuck that nigga* you've been cheating since 2001 when we first met and you sitting here going off about a jail letter. The way he acted showed me that he was doing his own thing.

He did not come home most of that weekend. He came home around 8:00 in the morning and he claimed he was at work. This had been his excuse for a while. I was tired of being last when it came to him. All this space and neglect from him will drive me into someone else's arms. Why do I always get stuck with the bullshit? I decided to think of myself. I had a habit of putting my feelings aside to make other people happy and comfortable. What about my happiness? What about me being comfortable? I just wanted someone to love me as much as I loved them. Is that so much to ask for? NO. The answer is no!!

It was time for me to go back on the ship. It was just as I thought it would be. I was glad I knew what to expect from being on the Dirty D. I knew that everyone would try to get at me. I was not interested in that kind of attention anymore. Reed knew a lot of people and Rich did too. I felt that both were out to get me. They wanted dirt on me so bad. I stayed to myself until I met Roberson on the USS Theodore Roosevelt. Roberson was a 5ft 11in tall chocolate 1st Class Officer. He was old school and smooth. He was not the finest man on the block, but he was attractive to me. I didn't know why, but I was always intrigued by older dudes. I think it was the way he spoke and how he carried himself. He was cool as fuck, and he made sure I had a good time.

Older dudes seemed like a challenge for me, and I was ready for a challenge. We were not feeling each other at first. We started spending a lot of time together and yes, I fucked him, and it was good. My husband was neglecting this pussy. He had five other pussies to worry about. I had caught him with so many women I lost count. He was too occupied to even care if I was cheating. Hell, it seemed like we were friends or roommates. I gave him a few months to not fuck me, give me attention, or make me happy. He chose not to. No excuses. I was doing something wrong, and I knew it was wrong.

I felt so bad afterward because it was amazing. He sucked my pussy until I squirted all over the place. We fucked and fucked and fucked. The dick was good, the mouth was good, everything was good. He knew what he was doing. He fucked my mind, body, and soul. The best thing about it was we knew what it was. We had feelings for one another, but we did not let it go too far. I did not want a recap of anything. Even though I wanted to leave Reed's ass I still did not want to get attached to anyone else. Robinson and I fucked in the officer's stake room, his house, and the car. We fucked anywhere.

We had a quick fling that lasted a short time. It was just a fuck. I was hurting and needed someone to make me feel good. I loved his touch. He was gentle with my body, and he made sure I bust a Nutt. Now that was something most men did not do. He had an old soul. I was 27 and he was about 37. NO ONE KNEW that we were fucking. So, when he started dating one of my friends I understood. I was all for them being in a relationship. She had no clue about us. She was stable, homebody, single, and she could give him what he wanted. I could not. I was married.

So, I respectfully fell back when they started dating. I focused on making my marriage work. I did not know how I was going to stop him from cheating or neglecting me. All I could do was try.

While on the ship, I stayed to myself and minded my business. I did not mess around with anyone else. I thought it could work if I just let him do whatever he wanted. I even invited my husband to our annual Christmas party. He came but did not want to. He was so upset that he missed a day at the club. It was so freaking sad.

Things started getting a little better for us. I wanted to have a baby. I wanted to get off this ship before there was a problem and Reed agreed Rich was being a stalker. I was treated differently by my supervisor. He moved me all over the ship to different places.

CHAPTER 16

I Have to Get Off This Ship

I wanted another baby and this time I would be married. Reed agreed to us having a baby, but it was like pulling teeth. Yeah, I know, we were not in a good place to have children together. We loved one another and were great friends so we made it work. I wanted a girl so I looked at the Chinese calendar to figure out the days that I would have a girl. We tried and tried. I was the one pushing this pregnancy. What was I thinking?

It seemed as if Reed wanted a baby, but he did not want the sex. He came from work with a thong on and I would try to have sex. He pretended he was asleep. I asked him, *why do you have a fucking thong on at work*? He said it helped with his nut sack. I knew he was lying. Hell, I already married his ass and there was no turning back now. I had made up my mind that getting a divorce was not an option. My first attempt failed. I was pregnant in my tubes, so they had to cancel the pregnancy and I had to get a Dilation and curettage. I was having a miscarriage. Unfortunately, I was sad for a few weeks.

Yes! We finally are pregnant again. GOODBYE SHIP! Once you become pregnant in the military you must get off the ship. I found out I was pregnant in May of 2008. I was so happy. I was sick as hell all day the next day. I went to the doctor, and I was 12 weeks pregnant. I wanted this baby, so I must do all the right things. No one had to worry about me doing anything to jeopardize my baby. I ate right and stayed off my feet. I was scared because I did not want the same thing to happen that happened to CJ.

I was ready for my baby girl. I was ready!! I already knew it was a girl and I was going to spoil her rotten. Honestly, I did not truly know what I was having. I researched online how to tell if it was a boy or girl. My entire pregnancy was miserable. I thought my husband would at least participate in something. I mean man, show some care and concern. He did not rub my belly, my feet, or go out to get my food cravings. I did everything alone.

I was discharging. I went to the doctor to get checked. Lord behold this nasty fuck had given me chlamydia. OH, HELL NO! That meant no more pussy for you, Reed! I was not about to catch shit else with this baby growing inside me. We did not fuck the entire pregnancy. I told him the only way he was getting any was if he wore a rubber. I knew he was fucking somebody else. I let you do what the fuck you wanted, but you should not have brought that shit home nigga. Have you lost your mind? And you had the nerve to get mad when I asked you to wear a condom. Safety was most important for me and my baby. I was not going to fuck him until after I had my daughter and after he showed me, that he could be faithful. I probably still would make him wear a condom.

I had Faith on Tuesday, December 30th, 2008, at 2:12 pm. I had a scheduled C-section due to me having Gestational Diabetes. I was so scared. Luckily for me, I did not have to take insulin shots. I was surprised because my sugar stayed high. The doctor stated that if I went full term, I would have a 10lb baby. My mother came down for the birth of my first baby girl and I was beyond excited. I told myself, I would love her and raise her in the right way. I would show her all the love that I craved as a child. Reed was there for the birth of our baby girl even though we were not on good terms.

Faith Ireanna Rogers was a beautiful yellow baby. She was taken to the NICU due to Jaundice. Jaundice is common in babies born before term. It is a condition when the skin is yellowing, and they must put the baby under a light. I wanted her with me the entire time, but they had to take her away. I did not like that. I knew it was best for her. I just relaxed and spent my time recovering from the C-section. Reed left to shower and take care of the house, so Mom and Tony B stayed with me.

Reed came back and he looked like he was dressed for the club. He had on a black suit, a tie, and a trench coat. He was ready for work. Mom looked at me and I looked at her. You could see the flames from her head. She was furious. She said to him "I know you are not about to leave your wife in this hospital bed after just having your baby to go to the club." I said mom *just let him go.* There was no need to get upset about it. Of course, he left. I did not see him until later the next day.

I still just wanted to make sure we both were happy. I was not happy at all. He was the one having all the fun. I think he knew how strongly I felt about marriage. He assumed I would never leave him especially now that I had a child with him. At the time leaving him was the last thing on my mind. I wanted a family badly. A few days later I left the hospital, and it was time for my only help to leave, my mom. I hated to see her leave because she helped me so much with the kids. One of his nephews told him that Faith was too light and may not be his. He should get a DNA test for Faith. TOO FUNNY!! One thing about me if I fuck around, I fuck around but when I get pregnant, I know who I fucked to get pregnant. This pregnancy was planned.

After six weeks, Reed and I went to see the doctor together to discuss a permanent form of birth control called tubal ligation. Reed and the doctor went back and forth about me having this procedure. He did not want me to get one for some reason. WHY? I had no clue. He asked the doctor if he had to sign for it and the doctor told him with her health no. She said if I got pregnant again I or the baby may not make it. My mind was made up. I did not want to have any more kids! Reed wanted to keep me pregnant or thought I was going to have more children. Not!!!! I was 28 years old. I knew I was a little young to get my tubes tied but I also knew I could not carry another child to term. Yes, I did want more children. Being pregnant was amazing!

I had three baby daddies already and that was enough. I had one in prison, one who didn't t want to have anything to do with his child, and another who is not acting as a father but as a hoe. So, NO I did not want any more kids. I was married and knew that I could become pregnant again. My bloodline alone played a factor in me easily becoming pregnant again. As Hargrove's were extremely fertile. Birth Control was not my friend and did not work for me. I did not take pills like I was supposed to. It was so hard to take pills every day at the same time. I even tried an IUD. I bled for two months straight. I spotted blood for a month or so and started bleeding again. The doctors said I was losing too much blood and they removed it.

Fast forward to today. Birth control today seems a little different and logical. Thinking back, I wish that I would have waited to tie my tubes. If I had decided to not get my tubes tied, I probably would have at least two more children. Which is not a good or bad thing because they would have been by my husband's. Maybe. I did not trust him, and he was back to his old tricks. I was committed to being a good girl until I left my nest. I had caught him so many times that I started to not care that he was cheating.

After I had healed from my C-section and was released from the doctors the military sent me new orders to leave. FUCK!!! I DID NOT WANT TO LEAVE MY BABIES WITH REED!!! He was so irresponsible and probably would leave the kids with anyone. Thank goodness my orders were for Bethesda, Maryland and I was so happy. I can finish my time here with my children. I believe Faith was about six months old with two little teeth. I was so proud of my accomplishments with my children. I did not want to leave them with anyone else. I had to leave and there was nothing that I could do about it.

I should not have left my children with someone who only cared about himself. I told him to not leave my children with anyone, but he did. He left them with anyone. He left them with a couple that lived across the street from us. Yes, we thought they were cool people but not cool enough for my kids to stay there without us. The father was a big guy, a Dallas Cowboys fan. He weighed about 400 pounds and his wife was in the military. She looked foreign. They had two boys and I think a little girl.

One day my son Donny told me that the older boy was making the younger boy have oral sex on him. I told Reed. I told his ass to not send my fucking children over there ever again. His ass had to still go to that fucking club no matter what. He talked with the father and he punked Reed's ass. He said his kids would never do any shit like that. Reed said to him "You know how women are, they believe everything the kids say." I HATE him for that shit so bad. This was the last straw. I knew I had to get out of the military because I did not trust "my husband with my children."

Sadly, some men do not have a caring bone in their bodies. You would think that all parents would have a sense of love for their children. I began to hate my husband!!! Now I knew for sure that we had a problem. He had a good talk game to convince me every time I got up the nerve to just say *you know what I am done.* I felt that I needed his help. I tried to do the right thing, but I was weak. I was hurting my children. I mean Reed coached football and basketball and never put Donny on the team. He did not want to do anything family oriented. We did not have any family portraits or any outing photos. Our family photos consisted of me and the kids. Reed knew he wasn't shit and will never be shit!!

CHAPTER 17

And I'm Out of Here

Well I was leaving the Navy. It was time. I was happy to leave with pride. I had been there for eight years, and I was tired. There was no telling where they were going to send me next. I will not have to leave my baby girl anywhere with anyone. This is a cruel world. I have a beautiful daughter and I will not allow anyone to strip her or disrespect her while I am here on earth. I cannot allow what has happened to me over the years to happen to her. So, YES! I decided to leave the military to take care of my children.

Reed had purchased our home and we were supposed to move there when I got out. May 1, 2009 was my last day. I packed my house out for us to move. Reed wanted us to stay in North Carolina with my mom until the house was finished. He said it was going to take a few months before the house would be ready. I was not sure if he told me the truth. Reed was a big liar. I was focused on getting my kids situated and in school. I enjoyed being with my family even though they would use what they could use. I wasn't as naive as before so there wasn't much to get. I stayed with my mom until our home was done.

My ex-KT got out of prison early and when I went home, he wanted to see me. I told him he could see me but that was it. I was focused on my family. I was not trying to get with him. I was not trying to go backward at all. We went out and had a good time. I limited everything because I knew I was going to leave to go to Atlanta soon.

Reed moved in with Devin, the gay couple who had the sex parties. He moved in with them to save more money. He continued working because it wasn't time for him to start his new job in Atlanta yet. I felt that Reed would do the right thing by his family now. I wanted him to. I begged him to do the right thing. I called him at all times of the night, and he would never answer. Every time we got on the phone, he would start an argument with me just to get off the phone and not talk for a few days.

One of his friends told me that I was wasting my time and I needed to move on. I did not want to move to North Carolina. Moving to Georgia would be good for me. A fresh start for our whole family. I knew I was lying to myself repeatedly. Why do I keep doing this? I did not want to hurt anymore. All I wanted was a happy family. I was not happy. I deserved to be happy. Maybe I was getting my Karma. No, that's not the case because I did not bother anyone intentionally. I was not going to let people treat me fucked up, and shit remains the same today! Do not do shit to me that you do not want to be done to you. PERIOD!!!

Reed started to act a little weird. Well, KT suggested that I drive to Maryland without Reed knowing; to see if he is the one for you. Mom joined in the conversation and asked me "Are you ready for what you are about to see?" You have a weak heart and I do not want you to go to jail if you see something you can't handle." I said mom *at this point I should be able to handle anything that I see. I have seen it all. I am ready to see what I need to see.* I rented a car and hit the road the next morning. I drove straight to Devin's house. Reed's truck was there.

I sat in the parking lot across the street from Devin's house. I was in disguise. I had a wig on, baggy clothes, and makeup. There was not much movement going on. I joined in with the cars that were already there at the strip mall. I dozed off a few times, but never longer than 30 minutes. I set my alarm. On the first night, I saw him pull out heading to work. It was about 9:00 p.m. on a Friday. He seemed so happy. He smiled while talking on the phone with someone. He didn't smile when he talked to me like that. He called me once that day to say, "I am headed to work, and I will call you tomorrow." I said, *ok cool.* I followed him to a live nightclub in DC. I got a great parking spot where I could see everything. I needed to see the door of the club and the parking lot of the club. The parking lot was fenced in, but you could see through the fence because of the missing wood.

A lot of the women in town knew him. He was popular with the ladies. They were all hugged up around him. He grabbed some of their asses. Most of the women were white or foreign. He groped them and one of them he kissed. I had a long lens camera to take pictures. He looked so happy. He had a huge smile on his face and boy was he looking really good with his tight-ass shirt on. Then

I saw him walk across the street with a girl. I got out of the car and walked over to the fence. He and the girl were kissing. He played in her ass and then she grabbed his dick. He fucked her right on the hood of her car and I watched the whole thing. AND no, I did not see him put on any protection.

She looked drunk as fuck and was falling all over the place. When he finished, he walked back to the club. I bet he smelled like shit because he did not clean himself off. He only used a few wipes the girl gave him by the car. She had a bag with all the hoe items that were needed. I was not mad because I already knew he was a serial cheater. I could only blame myself for dealing with this for so long. Loneliness and being naive thinking Reed would change made me stay. I thought he would eventually love me. Nahhh, he has not learned his lesson and I didn't think he would ever learn.

I drove to Devin's house early that morning and he was not home yet. He pulled in a few minutes later. He then got back in the car; I guess headed to the gym on the base. This is when shit got real. I called him. He sounded happy as hell. He said "hey baby how are you doing? How are my babies doing? I said *they are great. How are you?* He started lying about how boring work was. He went on with how he was dealing with a bunch of drunks and the VIP he had to deal with. I said *oh I know.* He confusingly said, "how do you know?" I said to him *You must think I am a fucking fool. I've been watching you and you have been bad. I just saw you pull into the base. You enjoy yourself sir, but just know I am here. I have been watching you for a few days.* I hung up.

I showered at Devin's house, and she watched me the entire time. Saying slick shit about how fine I was, and she asked about my tattoos. She insisted that I take a shower in her room even though she had four other rooms. Oh, and I just found out she and her wife were divorced. I got dressed and guess who pulled up Reed? He was on two wheels. Oh, he knew he was in some fucking trouble. I said to him *You no good mother fucker. I just don't understand why you cannot keep your dick in your pants. But you just gave me all that I needed, and I do not need you anymore.* He begged and pleaded. He gave me his normal excuse, "I did not do anything" he went on talking about how he would never hurt me, and he loved his wife. NIGGA FUCK YOU! I got in my car and pulled off. I was not gonna let him keep disrespecting me like this. I finally started to get it. Maybe I was not meant to be married.

I hit the highway in silence. I played a little music, and I cried just a little. I was not surprised because I felt he had been cheating. I guess I just needed to see it for myself. Now it was time for me to have some fun. I got back to mom's house, and she helped me take the rental car back. I still hoped that he would learn from this. The next weekend he came to North Carolina. I told him if I gave him any pussy, he would have to wear a condom. Then he had the nerve to say, "oh I know you fucking somebody else you always have." Yes, he turned it on me. He acted as if I was the one who got caught. He swore that he did not do anything and would not do anything to jeopardize his family. I told him I would not go with him to Atlanta unless he admitted to what the fuck he did. He admitted to fucking the girl on the side of the car when I told him I took pictures. The camera recorded it too. He said it was a trap and that the girl asked him to walk her to her car and she had a fuck bag. She had condoms, wipes, and everything needed for a fuck. I did not care anymore. I was about to be revengeful and fuck too. I fucked him and sent him on his way.

A few weeks later I finally gave my ex, KT some pussy and he loved it. KT did not have a big dick at all, but he knew what to do with it. He knew how to eat this pussy. He knew I was married. I enjoyed him and I did not feel bad at all. Why do niggas think they can fuck whoever and whenever they want to? This is not 1853 anymore. I was nobody's dummy. I will never allow anyone to have me looking stupid ever again. I don't care how long I am married or who I love. WHAT YOU DO TO ME I CAN DO TO YOU!! Do not do anything to me that you do not want to be done to you. I live by this. So, if you know me and you have done anything to me just know I have done something to you, and you just don't know it yet.

CHAPTER 18

Atlanta Bound

Yes, I did move to Atlanta. I had invested my money and time with this nigga. I had nothing. I was not able to save. The worst mistake I could have ever made was trusting this nigga. I made the mistake of not saving for myself. Trusting him to save for us. I had to get myself together. I need to save all my money and get my shit together to leave. I could see that this marriage was not going to work. I was still trying, and really thought the new move could change a few things. However, I knew this time would be a little different.

I will not let him know all my money moves. I will play my part for now. He's going to pay all the bills while I have a chance to save for once this time. I will have money saved up for when he starts his hoe shit again or when I decide to leave his ass. This time I will not deal with his bullshit. I was preparing myself for the shit show because I knew it was coming. I know I have done some bad things as revenge and there is no excuse for that. Whatever I did, I did for me. This move will be a new beginning. When the bullshit starts my bullshit will be worse. There is only so much a girl can take. Especially a girl like me. I had only one more try in me now.

I did not know anything about Atlanta. I only came here once to visit. I came to meet his family, but we did not do much sightseeing. When I finally moved to Atlanta, I was sad and depressed because I was alone. Reed worked at the club and fucked all the hoes. I did not like being the only one with our kids. I may as well have been a single parent. I learned that my kids were all that I needed. I was alone and he knew that. It seemed to give him some kind of power to know that I was alone.

I had no one to turn to. It almost seemed like this was his plan all along to get me away from my family and to himself. I looked on the bright side. I had a house, a family, and nice cars. I had everything I ever wanted. Something that I did not see often where I was from. The question remained: Was I happy? *Happiness is everything and I deserve to be happy* I think you guys all know the answer to that. NO! I was not happy at all, and I still did not have a voice. I even let people tell me how to decorate my home because they said my style was country.

I had let it get to the point again. I allowed him to do whatever he wanted. I knew that shit was going to happen when he started working at the nightclubs in Atlanta. WOW!! He had not learned his lesson and I was dumb enough to let him keep getting away with it. Nothing was enough. I even fucked other women with him, but he was never satisfied. I know you are asking why not just leave. It is easier said than done. Anyone on the outside looking in can say "just leave a relationship" especially if you are getting abused. IT IS NOT THAT EASY! I couldn't leave yet. I had worked so hard to get here. I let him save all our money and get this house. I had nothing. I couldn't just get up and leave. I did not want to go back to North Carolina with nothing to show for me being in the military for so long. No, I was staying. This time around I had a plan, and I will show him that I was stronger than he thought I was.

I stayed in the house with the kids all day and all night. I made sure the house was clean, kids were dressed for school, they ate, they showered, and did their schoolwork. I even made sure my husband had a meal almost every night. I was a wife. I paid all my bills, bought groceries, and saved the rest of my money. Reed paid all the household bills. I had to think smart this time. I knew it was about to be some bullshit because he never took me anywhere. I only went to the grocery store and some of the Camp Creek shopping areas around. Everything we needed was there.

It was the same shit all over again. I had concluded that I was not enough. I believe I had become comfortable with being a housewife. I let myself go. Reed became comfortable with me not nagging him. I allowed him to fuck around and still had a home cooked meal waiting for him. I gave him pussy whenever he wanted. He was very comfortable with doing the same bullshit that he always did. But I had a trick for his ass this time. I was not going to sit around anymore. I was not going to put up with his shit any longer.

Don't get me wrong we had a great sex life whenever he was not distracted by other women. I was not a boring person in bed. I gave him every possible sexual experience there was. I remember one time we were having sex and I noticed something different about him. I could not put my finger on it but whatever it was it kind of turned me on. I don't know why but it did. He was taking a shower and I decided to join him. I started to kiss him and stroke his dick. I jacked him off. I don't know what made me take a chance to start playing with his ass. But I did. He did not stop me, so I kept fingering his ass. He moaned and it turned me on a little more, so I continued. As I jacked him off and fingered his ass he began to moan louder, and he burst off like he never did before. It was amazing. Especially for him.

I do not know why he wanted to fuck with anyone else. I guess there were things he wanted to do with them that he did not want me to know. That day had me curious to learn what he was really into, and I was willing to explore with him. We even went to the Trampeze which was a place where people went to find other people to spice up their relationship or just fuck other people. Well, I did allow him to fuck another girl while we were there. She was skinny and he seemed to enjoy it and it did not bother me because we had done shit like this in Maryland. Again, why cheat when you know your wife is with all the shits if that is what you want to do?

We did have a great sexual lifestyle whenever he wanted his wife to be a part of it. I did not like him turning to other women for sex and attention. I didn't mind sharing if I knew what was going on. I hated to find out something on my own or from someone else. I wanted to be able to trust my man enough to be able to tell whoever I *already know what my husband is doing, or I already knew that*. I did not want to be looking stupid. He did not want me to know what he was doing but he wanted to know what I was doing.

I decided to go to cosmetology school. We had to put Faith in daycare now. I was so excited about going to school. The military paid for my education. I was so excited about starting hair school at Empire Beauty School in Kennesaw, Georgia. I wanted to learn how to keep myself up and of course my baby girl as well. I also wanted to meet new people and start networking. I had to do something, and this was Atlanta, the capital of hair and business. I started school on

May 12, 2011, I was so excited and so ready to start school. I had tried several other Empire schools close to where I lived, but this one stood out. I was accepted with open arms. I was willing to drive 45 minutes every day to attend school, and that's just what I did.

Before I started school, I went back to North Carolina often to hang out with my dad Nate, and my cousins. I missed them and I did not have any friends. My dad talked me into having parties. He said I could make some money. Of course, I had haters and some of the parties didn't work out. I made more money at the house party than anything. I had a great time. I even had Reed come help with one of the parties. It was cool, but nothing like the parties in Atlanta. I came home every other weekend. The kids were always with me. Reed did not take care of the kids or watch them ever. I felt wanted and needed there with my family. However, I knew I could not stay there forever. I had to go back home to Atlanta. It was time for me to focus on myself and get myself together.

Reed did not like me leaving the house because he loved the control, he had over me. He only wanted me to hang with people he knew. He wanted me to hang out with his nephew's girlfriend. She was cool as shit. I guess he felt if I hung out with her, she would let him, or her boyfriend know what I was doing. I did hang out with her. She immediately knew we had problems. I was not thinking about anybody or anything else. I just wanted to have a little fun, party, dance, and have a few drinks. I was the type of person who easily trusted people. I wanted friends and I didn't care who they were at the time. She did not tell Reed anything we did. I was able to have fun around her, but I knew that anything that I did wrong could get back to Reed. This was the start of me getting a taste of Atlanta.

I met a guy named Keith at the club and he seemed to be a baller or whatever. I ignored him at first, but we began to talk, and he did not seem interested in me at all. He seemed to have women all over him. I was interested. I let him know that I was married. The next time I saw him at the club we exchanged numbers. We started meeting up and he gave me the attention that Reed was not giving. Keith made me feel beautiful and special. I will forever be grateful for him giving me a self-esteem boost. I knew someone else wanted me and I didn't have to keep dealing with Reed's SHIIT!!!!!!!!!! He was not my only option.

It was time for school. I had to focus. Oh, Did I mention that Reed's nephew's girlfriend Tina was a hairstylist, and she was pretty good. She did my hair a few times and I loved it. School was my focus now and I was so excited because this was the start of my new journey. Focused!!!! It was wonderful here and I think that I will love it here. The school was in a strip mall in Kennesaw Georgia. There were other things there to do on break. I learned so many things while going to school. I tried new things because everything was in the strip mall. I ate sushi for the first time. It was pretty good.

Fast forward to today and I still love me some sushi. I got my first wax from a place in the strip mall while I was there. It was a horrible experience. They used the same wax that they used for eyebrow waxing, which ripped the skin off my *fatty patty,* and it was painful. I said to myself, *I will never again get another wax.* I ate at different restaurants and shopped at different cool places. I found another mall around the corner called Cumberland Mall. It was huge. I stopped there often to buy shit that I knew I didn't need. I bought shit to make myself look good. My childhood trauma was creeping up again. I still did not think I was pretty. I was still insecure. Reed did not make it better. He made me feel like I was never enough. I had to lack something. He had family, friends, and hoes here. He never got lonely because found entertainment with something or someone. I had no one.

My school process was easy, and I was ready. I was ready for something new to add to my nail tech license. I wanted to start my shit and become my own person. I was nervous around so many new people. There were a lot of gay people in my program. I was not used to hanging out with them. It was more gay guys than girls. I only had met one gay guy on the ship. I knew Reed's friends Devin and her wife, but we didn't hang out much. My new friends and I hung out regularly. These were my friends, and it was different. Different in a good way. I met most of everyone I knew from Reed.

I met people that taught me and treated me with respect. Most of them were gay, bi, lesbians, or just free spirits. First, there was Reggie, the twerk queen. He was only 18. He was real as fuck and fun to be around. Then there was Greg. He was from Chicago, and he was great as well. He performed at drag shows and was an entertainer. We hung out at gay clubs because we wanted to support him. He was very outspoken and told it like it was to whoever. He cursed your ass out at any time. It didn't matter if he was right or wrong because he would shut your ass down. He could dance his ass off too. I also met Greg's husband Brandon. He was cool and very humble. He seemed shy at first but later opened up. He was just a nice guy. Oh wait, there was more. I was excited to have friends. I had been alone for so long. Okay, so there was Candy. She and I became close after cosmetology school. She introduced me to a lot of things. Keep reading to learn what I am talking about.

I met Katina through Greg. I found out she was from the same area of North Carolina I was from. We hit it off right away and are still friends today. We even kissed once. She was a strong-willed woman and a real piece of work. She would put you in your place quick. Katina introduced me to the real wax, the lady was a real Brazilian woman. I felt as if it was the best thing I had ever done. I never felt my pussy feel so smooth. Then there was Denise. She was an awesome individual from St. Louis. She was kind, nice, loving, caring, and always willing to help. Overall, she was a great person and she never switched up. I never saw her mad or fussing. I loved her for being herself. She was spunky. She did not have a shy bone in her body. Her vocabulary was different but proper. We had an amazing time. She was a GREAT friend. Overall, she was a great person and she never switched up.

Then there was Patrice. She was a great person that loved her kids. But we did not stay friends for long. She was nice and caring at times, but mostly cared only about herself. Patrice was a little confused about herself. She wanted to be like a stud, but she liked dick too. One day she would be a stud then the next day she would be all girly. She didn't know what she wanted. This was the start of me becoming me. And me living my own life. I had my own group of friends.

I enjoyed school and had a great time. I learned so many things here. My teacher Mrs. Church was awesome. She kept me under her wings the entire time. I attended her church often too. She was an awesome teacher and a wonderful friend. I was not good at doing hair in the beginning, but I did learn. Natural hair was my thing, and I was good at it. I was good at natural hair, lashes, and nails. I loved meeting new people. I loved being free, having friends, going out, partying, and building for myself. I was having the best time ever. I was FALLING IN LOVE WITH ME! I began to learn my worth. Why was I even in this marriage? I deserved more. He didn't even want me. I saw a change in him when I started school. I was now making new friends and focusing on myself.

CHAPTER 19

The Shit Hit the Fan

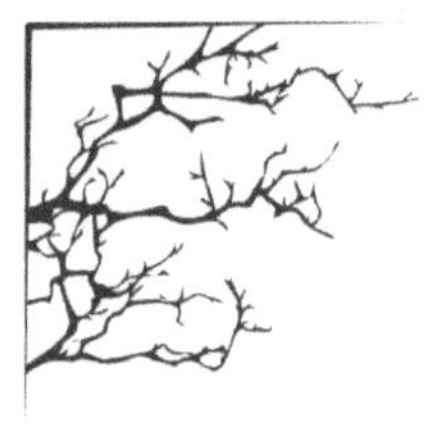

I went to North Carolina one weekend to visit my Aunt Dot. She was a very heavy set bright red lady who kept me smiling all the time. I checked on her and my dad because they both were not in the best of health. We had drinks and had a great time together. She was a heavy drinker and I guess it was to ease the pain. I believe that's why I drank so much; to ease the pain. I was looking for attention because I was not getting any at home. But I did not want to deal with anyone from my hometown. I knew almost everyone there and most did not want anything out of life. I was not trying to go down that rabbit hole.

I had been in North Carolina all weekend and now it was time to go. I loved chilling on the front porch and feeling the breeze. It was so peaceful. I am a laid-back chill person. I just wanted to be happy. My head was not in a good space right now. But I knew I had to go home. I was supposed to leave early but I was enjoying my time with my Auntie. I was not looking forward to this six-hour drive. I had driven back to my hometown several times lately and had gotten used to it. I called Reed around 9:00 pm to let him know that I was on my way home.

He had been fussing earlier about me coming to North Carolina so much. He expected me earlier. He fussed and told me that the kids had school and did not need to miss days. Suddenly, his tune changed. He was all nice and said "I know you want to spend time with your family. One more night won't hurt, and they can miss one day out of school. Don't rush home, it's too dark." He yawned as if he was tired and ready to go to bed. I knew Reed like a book. I knew he was faking.

When I explained it to my aunt she looked really confused. Her ill husband sat in his chair outside with us. He asked me "Are you ready to see what your husband is doing?" I looked at him confused. My expression was like *what are you talking about*? He said "If you want to know what your husband is doing, go home right now. I heard you saying that you don't care what he is doing. You know he is lying, and you feel bad about everything you do here because you care about his feelings. Go see for yourself. It will be different if you catch someone in the home you share with him. You then will see how much he really loves you." He looked at me and said, "get your babies and go home now." I called Reed back and told him I was going to take his advice and come home in the morning. He yawned and said he was going back to bed and that he would call me in the morning.

I packed up my car and strapped the kids in and we were on the road within the next hour. It was a six-hour ride and I left at 11 pm. It was dark as hell, but I had to get home. I was praying the whole way for God to reveal what he wanted me to see. I was ready to be free from all this hurt. I asked God to, *please show me if he is for me or if he is not for me.* I prayed all the way. I almost fell asleep a few times. I smoked a black and mild all the way to stay up and I drank four red bulls. I ate snacks, my heart was beating the whole way because deep down I knew something was wrong. I was flying. I drove 80+ miles all the way home. Faith was about two at the time. She and CJ slept the whole ride. But my oldest son kept waking up, and he kept asking me "Ma are you okay?" He did this throughout the ride.

I got home around five in the morning. I pulled into the garage, and I saw my Sonata. His truck was in the shop, and he drove my car. I let the garage down and told the kids to stay in the car and don't move. Of course, Donny was smart as hell and asked me if I was ok. I said to him, *"Listen, son, no matter what I need you to stay in the car and watch your sister and brother.* He said, "ok ma I will stay right here."

When I opened the door, the alarm chirped and that was the first red flag because he would never sleep without the alarm set. He was so adamant about the alarm being set no matter what time of day. So, it was kind of weird that the alarm was not set. The basement door was wide open with a second red flag. I walked in and headed to my bedroom and here comes Reed, sliding down the hallway butt booty naked wet. I walked past him thinking that maybe someone was in my room. I looked in the closet and all the kids' rooms and there was nobody. He got dressed real fucking quick and he showed me a hanger and said, "I'm going to put this in the car, so it won't get wrinkled."

He kept repeating I'm going to work. I am headed to work. I said, *Okay.* He kept trying to explain himself. I laughed and said to him, *you think I'm stupid huh.* He asked me to walk the dog and walk her in the backyard. I said *NO!* Why would I walk a dog in the backyard when the house is fenced? I asked him, *when have I ever walked a dog?* I headed towards the basement and walked down the stairs. It had a funny smell. It smelled like sex, weed, and pussy. As soon as I hit the last step, I felt something was up. He tried his best to get me out of the basement. I looked everywhere and the guest bedroom door was locked. I knew someone was in this room. *I mean why would the door be locked?* I heard my kids come into the house and someone had to pee, so I headed back upstairs and told the boys to get dressed for school. Let's see how whoever was in my house going to get the fuck up out of here; without getting their ass beat. My husband was so scared because he knew what I was capable of.

YES, he should be very afraid.................. THE DANGER OF A MAD ASS TAURUS!!!

TO BE CONTINUED......

My Truth

Please do not be sad when people are removed from your life. Understand that it is a part of God's plan. He removes certain people out of your life to BLESS you, TEACH you, and PRE-PARE you for what he has in store for you. Some people are in your life wasting space, discouraging you, making you doubt yourself, or destroying your character. LET THEM GO!!! They are only turning you away from your purpose and destiny. God did not intend for them to be a part of your journey.

Some people are not meant for your blessings. The blessing is for YOU not for them. You see, they are holding your blessings from coming in for you. God will remove these individuals from your life, and he does not care how he must remove them or what problems he allows to remove them. HE WILL remove them. DO NOT WORRY about how they are removed.

They are not your people, and they mean you harm. Listen to God's PROTECTION. God only wants to bless you and the people who are connected to you.

Not only will this be a lesson for you, but it will make you stronger. Use your life lessons as God's way of equipping you for greatness. God is preparing you. God must make sure you are ready

for all the blessings coming your way. Life is a journey, and it takes time to be prepared for what God has for you. So be ready!!!!!
Felicia Hargrove

About the Author

Felicia Hargrove was born in Durham, North Carolina. She was raised in both Townsville and Henderson, North Carolina. She currently resides in Riverdale, Georgia.

She has a Bachelor of Arts Degree in Criminal Justice. She is the founder and owner of Image of Faith FSH LLC.

She has a strong passion for teaching, mentoring, and counseling young adolescent children.
Felicia has been writing for 20+ years: Loose Lips Sink Ships is her first published book.

She served in the United States Navy for a decade, as a Boatswain's mate and Culinary Specialist. She worked passionately with the local sheriff's office for five years.

She is a dedicated mother and wife. She quotes, "My family is everything."